GUSTAV MAHLER

DERYCK COOKE

GUSTAV MAHLER
An Introduction to his Music

FABER MUSIC
in association with
FABER & FABER

First published in 1980 by
Faber Music Ltd in association with
Faber and Faber Ltd,
3 Queen Square, London WC1N 3AU
Second Edition 1988
Designed by M. & S. Tucker
Printed in Great Britain

British Library Cataloguing in Publication Data

Cooke, Deryck
Gustav Mahler: an introduction to his music — 2nd ed.
1. Mahler, Gustav — Criticism and interpretation
I. Title
780'.92'4   ML410.M23
ISBN 0-571-10087-2

CONTENTS

PREFACE TO FIRST EDITION

THIS book has its origin in a booklet which Deryck Cooke wrote for the BBC for publication in 1960, as a companion to the BBC's celebrations of the centenary of Mahler's birth. In fact, the introductory essay, 'Mahler as Man and Artist', is taken direct from that text – written at a time when it was still possible to talk of the 'growing recognition of Mahler's stature also moving forward in Germany and Spain, and beginning even in France and Italy'. The remainder of the original text, dealing with Mahler's music, has been considerably expanded: we have been able to draw on programme notes and articles which Deryck Cooke wrote in more recent years, where he was able to discuss individual works in greater depth than was permitted by the scope of his BBC commission.

A glance through the pages will show that each symphony has been dealt with in three sections: a brief opening paragraph giving dates of composition and first performance, orchestration, etc.; an essay; and a description. While it is hoped that the book as a whole will give an illuminating picture of Mahler both as a composer and as the very human being who was that composer, it is intended primarily as a kind of handbook, which can be easily referred to before or after listening to the music itself. We have also included the texts of all Mahler's vocal works, together with English translations. These translations are by Deryck Cooke, except for the *Lieder und Gesänge* by Berthold Goldschmidt and Colin Matthews, *Das klagende Lied* by David Matthews, and Part 11 of Symphony No. 8 where Louis MacNeice's translation of the closing scene from Goethe's *Faust* has been used.

The editing of this book has been a joint project; and the appearance of our names below should not imply that we bear a greater responsibility for it than our collaborators, Berthold Goldschmidt and Hazel Smalley.

Colin Matthews
David Matthews

PREFACE TO SECOND EDITION

FOR this new edition, no changes have been made to the text, since Deryck Cooke's insights into Mahler's music remain as fresh today as when they were written. Some small revisions have been made to the translations. Although the attribution to Li-Tai-Po of 'Der Einsame im Herbst' and 'Von der Jugend' from *Das Lied von der Erde* has been kept here, Donald Mitchell has recently revealed in the third volume of his study of Mahler, *Songs and Symphonies of Life and Death*, that these poems are almost certainly not based on Chinese originals, but are in all probability pieces of *Chinoiserie* by Judith Gautier. In fact the whole background to the Bethge translations that Mahler used in *Das Lied* is much more complicated than was hitherto supposed.

Mahler research has continued apace since 1980. Much new biographical material has emerged in Henry-Louis de La Grange's definitive biography, the second and third volumes of which still await an English edition. One musical discovery may briefly be mentioned here: a Symphonic Prelude for orchestra has come to light which, though it was first attributed to Mahler's friend Rudolf Krzyzanowski, on stylistic grounds seems much more likely to have been one of Mahler's student orchestral works. More information about the piece may be found in the revised edition of Donald Mitchell's *Gustav Mahler: The Early Years*.

It is now over ten years since Deryck Cooke's untimely death. During this period, perhaps his greatest achievement, his performing version of Mahler's Tenth Symphony, has become widely known through steadily increasing numbers of performances, and several recordings. It has now entered the consciousness of almost all who love Mahler's music, and to consider Mahler's life's work without it would now be unthinkable. It is pleasing to recall here that it was the BBC's commission to write the centenary booklet that first led Deryck Cooke to investigate the sketches of the Tenth, and to discover that, contrary to received opinion, they could be realized and played.

David Matthews

MAHLER
AS MAN AND
ARTIST

MAHLER AS MAN AND ARTIST

THE belated recognition of Mahler as one of the great symphonists is among the most remarkable features of our post-war musical life. To understand why it was so long delayed, we must get a clear historical perspective. Mahler, born in 1860, belonged to the generation of Sibelius and Richard Strauss; but he died in 1911, aged only fifty, whereas Strauss died in 1949, aged eighty-five, and Sibelius in 1957, aged ninety-one.

During their long lives, these two composers saw their music overcome early opposition to its 'modernity' and enter the normal concert repertory. Sibelius, the independent, is recognized in this country as an outstanding figure in twentieth-century music; this is largely due to the persistent advocacy of conductors, notably Bantock, Wood and Beecham, for in countries where his music has found no conductor-advocate, musical opinion has never caught up with him. Strauss, the last great romantic, is recognized everywhere as a leading composer of the twentieth century; the advocate largely responsible for this was he himself, though his music was soon taken up by conductors the world over. Thus Strauss and Sibelius have been familiar for half a century, and are now inevitably suffering from the swing of fashion: in an age which has repudiated its immediate predecessors, they are being written off by the characteristic contemporary musician – rather prematurely, one feels.

The case of Mahler is entirely different. In many ways more forward-looking then either Strauss or Sibelius, he encountered much stronger opposition; nevertheless, he was winning his cause as a composer with his own baton, when death cut off his promised development into a twentieth-century figure. His music was eventually accepted in Vienna, due to the advocacy of his disciple Bruno Walter; in Holland and Belgium it is extremely popular – a legacy of the Mahler festivals given by Willem Mengelberg; and in America, since Bruno Walter settled there, it has won favour. But elsewhere, until recently, it found no persistent advocate, and consequently no recognition.

In England, Sir Henry Wood presented four of the symphonies before 1914, but this small seed did not take root. The war intervened, and Mahler became a forgotten 'lesser romantic'. In the twenties, the critics, full of the new English school and the new anti-romantic reaction, began to attack Wagner and Strauss; they could hardly damage the reputation of these composers, but they did prevent any further Germanic romantics from being accepted. When the enthusiasm of a conductor (usually Wood) brought a Mahler symphony to performance, the press mainly voiced the spirit of the age, dismissing the work with contempt. Understandably, few concert promoters cared to engage huge forces to perform works too unpopular to guarantee an adequate box-office return – yet how could they become popular unless they were frequently performed? Mahler's name disappeared into musical dictionaries, usually heading an ill-informed, derogatory article.

This situation persisted until the end of the last war. But since then, Mahler's music has become more generally available, thanks to the BBC, the recording companies, the growing advocacy of conductors, and the open-minded attitude of a new generation of critics; and it has captured the public imagination, drawing full houses and receiving prolonged ovations. Of whom does this public consist? Largely of ordinary music-lovers, who enjoy great music, whether by Bach, Mahler or Stravinsky, once they have the chance to discover it; and of young musicians who, unaffected by the dated polemics of anti-romanticism, are prepared to judge a 'romantic' composer on his merits. This growing recognition of Mahler's stature is also moving forward in Germany and Spain, and beginning even in France and Italy. Mahler, widely scoffed at in his own day, declared, firm in the conviction of his genius: 'My time will come'. It seems that it *has* come – a hundred years after his birth, and nearly fifty years after his death.

*

A contributory factor has been the favourable attitude of certain modern composers. Some, like Schoenberg, Berg and Britten, have expressed unstinted admiration; but others have given only qualified approval, admitting Mahler's status as an important historical figure. Aaron Copland, for example, in *Our New Music* (1941), sees clearly the paradox that of all the romantics, this arch-romantic 'had most to give to the music of the future'. He says: 'Two facets of his musicianship were years in advance of his time. One was the curiously contrapuntal fabric of the musical texture, the other, more obvious, his strikingly original instrumentation. Viewed properly, these two elements are really connected. It was because his music was so contrapuntally conceived . . . that his instrumentation possesses that sharply-etched and clarified sonority that may be heard again in the music of later composers. . . . Unusual combinations of instruments, sudden unexpected juxtapositions of sonorities, thinly-scored passages of instruments playing far apart in their less likely registers – all such effects are to be found again in the orchestral works of Schoenberg, Honegger, Shostakovich, or Benjamin Britten.'

Others have noticed how Mahler's harmonic explorations advanced the disruption of tonality begun in Wagner's *Tristan* towards the early free atonality of Schoenberg. Moreover, his method of 'constant variation' looks forward to serial procedures; the linear counterpoint of the Rondo-Burleske of the Ninth Symphony foreshadows Hindemith, and its wry modulations anticipate Prokofiev. Mahler was a focal point of the age: he stepped up the psychological tension in romanticism until it exploded into the violent patterns of 'our new music'.

All this is very true and interesting; but to regard Mahler as a mere predecessor is to ignore ninety per cent of his significance – to make the mistake of the romantics who saw Mozart purely as the 'precursor of romanticism'. Mahler is an outstanding composer in his own right: the foreshadowings in his music are only fascinating by-products of its own original genius, which often enough foreshadows very little. Aaron Copland sensed this: 'When all is said, there remains something extraordinarily touching about the man's work, something that makes one willing to put up with the weaknesses. Perhaps this is because his music is so very Mahler-like in every detail. All his nine symponies are suffused with personality – he had his own way of saying and doing everything. The irascible scherzos, the heaven-storming calls in the brass, the special quality of his communings with nature, the gentle melancholy of a transitional passage, the gargantuan Ländler, the pages of an incredible loneliness – all these, combined with his histrionics, an inner warmth, and the will to evoke the largest forms and the grandest musical thoughts, add up to one of the most fascinating composer-personalities of modern times.'

Yes, there is something strangely compelling about Mahler. He was, it is being realized, a great composer with something entirely new and significant to say. But his case is peculiarly difficult: he was a romantic, and therefore suspect; but he was a romantic with a difference, which complicates matters considerably. This 'difference' – what was entirely new and original in his music – has nothing to do with romanticism as such, but still seems to many as odd and impermissible as in his own day. However, it is the very stuff of his genius, and until it is understood, his music will still continue to perplex. Again, we must see the problem in its historical perspective.

During the twenties and thirties, the romantics were derided for using music to express 'extra-musical' ideas, and their stature was measured by the classical yardstick of 'pure music'. The attitude still persists, but now that the revolution is over in the creative sphere, it is possible to take a more objective historical view of the romantics: to realize that we are just as misguided in condemning them for their greatest achievement – the extension of music's expressive power to voice to the full the discontents, longings and aspirations of humanity – as they were in depreciating the classics for *their* greatest achievement – the elevation of music on to the highest plane of pure beauty. Expression of feeling is an integral part of romanticism; to repudiate this element is to ignore the music's true signficance. We are always led back from technical and aesthetic considerations to the question 'What does the music express?' – and thence to the composer himself, as a man. What sort of a man was Mahler?

＊

First of all, he was a late romantic. But what exactly is a romantic, and further, a late one? Romanticism has many facets: at its best it is an exploration of the wonder and mystery of life, and of the powerful unconscious urges which impel human action; at its worst, an addiction to vague mystification and turgid sentimentality. But ignoring side-issues, romanticism was ultimately this: the liberation of man's confined spirit, at the time of the French Revolution, after centuries of tyrannical restraint on freedom of thought, feeling, and action. For the first time men were free to vent their long-suppressed yearnings and aspirations; to discover what man was and what he might become; to create their own destiny according to natural human needs and desires.

In music, the first proud mood of confidence was supremely voiced by Beethoven: the Eroica, the Fifth, the 'Choral', *Egmont* and *Fidelio* blazed a trail of humanistic optimism from 1803 to 1824. Unfortunately, the new world delayed, and disillusionment followed. Wagner conceived his Siegfried as 'the new man of the communistic paradise'; but the 1848 German revolution failed, and Siegfried went under in *The Twilight of the Gods* (completed in 1873). The doubt had arisen – could man achieve his ends? God, as Nietzsche said, was dead; man was now his own god; but could he attain to a god's fullness of being and fashion a perfect world? There followed the 'world-weariness' of the later romantics: discouraged by the failure of too-eager hopes they withdrew into imaginary paradises, to nurse their unfulfilled longings. In Strauss's *Ein Heldenleben* (1898), the hero retreats into bitter-sweet resignation; Strauss, Delius and others lamented poignantly the sunset of the romantic ideal.

But since then, new tyrannies and new wars have shaken Europe, and we find ourselves the uneasy heirs of the first romantics, still committed to their ideal of refashioning the world, though more soberly in view of bitter experience. Their central problem – the discrepancy between human aspiration and human weakness – is still ours, manifest in Europe's powerlessness to fulfil boundless potentialities for progress, owing to the diversion of human energy into preparations for a possible war of annihilation.

Of all the late romantics, Mahler speaks most clearly to our age. An heir of Beethoven and Wagner, he was intensely preoccupied with this discrepancy between aspiration and weakness. His persistent theme is 'The spirit is willing, but . . .' – no, not 'the flesh is weak'; rather, the spirit is willing, but is undermined by its own fatal weakness – faced by life's frustrations, it is a prey to discouragement, bitterness, emptiness, despair. This general human dilemma was acute in Mahler's case, as we can see by considering him as an individual.

Mahler was born on 7 July 1860. His father was a Jewish innkeeper in the Bohemian village of Kalischt (now Kalište); shortly after Mahler's birth, the family moved to the nearby town of Iglau (now Jihlava). Bohemia was then part of the Austro-Hungarian Empire; Mahler's native tongue was German, and he ranked as an Austrian subject of Jewish descent. He was thus from the beginning affected by racial tensions: he belonged to an unpopular Austrian minority among Bohemians, and to an unpopular Jewish minority within the Austrian one. Throughout his life, he felt a sense of exile. He once said: 'I am thrice homeless, as a native of Bohemia in Austria, as an Austrian amongst Germans, as a Jew throughout the world. Always an intruder, never welcomed.' And when faced with an unpleasant situation, he would fall back smilingly on a favourite quotation: 'Who hath brought me into this land?'

Then there was the intensely unhappy family background of his childhood. The brutal father ill-treated the delicate mother, creating a father-hatred and a mother-fixation in Mahler himself; despite the family's poverty, the mother bore fourteen children; seven died in infancy, five of them when Mahler was a growing boy. When he was thirteen, his favourite brother Ernst, one year younger than himself, died after a long illness; and Mahler saw it through to the end, sitting for hours by his bed, telling him stories. Of those who survived, Alois grew up to be a crazy character, wildly parading delusions of grandeur; Otto, musically gifted, shot himself at the age of twenty-one.

Looking at Mahler in his childhood, we see a moody, introspective boy, with short spare figure and worried eyes, roaming the countryside and wondering how a world so fresh and beautiful can contain so much cruelty. We see him day-dreaming, listening to the fascinating sounds that echo around the landscape: cries of birds and indeterminate noises of nature, country song and dance, bugle-calls and tattoos from a nearby barracks. All these were later to be woven into his songs and symphonies.

He showed an early aptitude for music, picking out tunes on the piano as a child, and it was as a pianist that he first made his mark, with a recital in Jihlava at the age of ten. Skipping over his schooldays, we see him next as a youth in Vienna, studying at the Conservatoire. Outwardly, he is a normal (if specially gifted) student: he wins piano and composition prizes; revolts against authority and indulges in the customary pranks; gets to know Bruckner, a man of fifty-odd teaching at the University, and Hugo Wolf, a fellow-student with whom he shares rooms. But tension still surrounds him: his two closest friends are both mentally unstable (one, Hans Rott, a talented composer, later died in an asylum, as did Wolf). Mahler's inner preoccupation with the riddle of existence, the inescapable facts of cruelty, pain and death, persists. He seeks an answer in German romantic literature, in the philosophy of Schopenhauer and Nietzsche, and above all in the music of Beethoven and Wagner. In his darkest moments, he contemplates suicide.

Fortunately, life claimed him. His tension, never to be resolved, found an outlet in activity. Such was the wealth of his nature that this activity had to be twofold – creative and re-creative, composing and conducting; and he pursued both callings with heart and soul. No other musician, except Wagner, possessed in such equal measure the introvert's capacity for self-absorption, the extrovert's capacity for self-assertion, and the iron will to weld them together and force them to do its purpose.

What preserved him was his genius as a composer, which flowered in *Das klagende Lied*, before he ever thought of being a conductor. At the age of twenty, Mahler was a composer and a pianist; but he obtained his first badly-needed job as conductor at the theatre of an Austrian health resort, taking up the baton from sheer necessity. He was never to lay it down again: although he often cursed the drudgery of a conductor's life, it obviously fulfilled an inner need, for he continued it long after it was materially necessary. During the first part of his career, he was dogged by the necessity of providing for his brothers and sisters; nevertheless, we see him slowly climbing the ladder of fame, moving from subordinate positions in provincial Austrian and German towns to important posts in Hamburg and Budapest, until at thirty-seven he reaches the very height of ambition – the Directorship at the Vienna Opera.

Still slight of physique, still idealistic of temperament, still haunted by dark questionings, he has acquired a keen, sceptical intellect, a terse ironic wit, and an extraordinary power of command. Flashing his piercing eyes through his glasses, and impatiently gnawing his lower lip, the man seems to be driven by a demon. Absorbed in his study, he penetrates to the inmost heart of the great masterpieces; in theatre and concert hall he strives ruthlessly for perfect performances of them, riding roughshod over the usual slackness and lack of imagination, sparing neither himself nor anyone else. Making enemies right and left by his utter indifference to personal considerations, he nevertheless exerts such a spell over singers, players and technicians alike that he achieves matchless realizations of the works of the great masters. As a conductor he becomes a legend in his own lifetime.

But all this only in the winter months. Every summer, retiring to the heart of the Austrian countryside, he bends his apparently inexhaustible energy to what is, after all, the real task of his life – the creation of an entirely new kind of music: vast symphonies in which the riddle of human existence shall find at once a full statement and a resolution. Then in the autumn, with a symphony fully sketched, back to the routine of the opera-house, any spare time from which is devoted to the labour of completing the symphony in full score. Small wonder that this man, living two full lives and never taking a proper holiday, should find his heart failing before he was fifty. We see him in his last years burning out before his time, knowing he is soon to die. Forced to leave Vienna in 1907, owing to official and public antagonism (fomented by anti-Semitism), he goes to America to conduct the New York Philharmonic Orchestra and the Metropolitan Opera Company; but he still returns to Austria each summer to compose his last works. He died in Vienna on 18 May 1911, fifty days before his fifty-first birthday.

*

To understand Mahler's personality, we have to set it in its proper framework – that of the 'great artist', as the term was understood in the nineteenth century. A 'great artist' was more than a composer, a painter or a poet: in an age which had lost faith in religious doctrines, and felt the need of human prophets, he was a kind of superman, a far-seeing visionary with a mission and a message. To this category belonged such various figures as Wagner, Flaubert, Rodin and Rilke – men who devoted their whole vital power to artistic creation, leaving neither time nor energy for the affairs of everyday life. Mahler, like all 'great artists', shouldered humanity's burden and took himself very seriously. What he felt and thought about life, and expressed in his music, seemed to him of the utmost consequence, and he was accustomed to having it regarded in this light: after the first performance of the Eighth Symphony, Thomas Mann wrote to Mahler, calling him 'the man who, as I believe, expresses the art of our time in its profoundest and most sacred form'. Like Wagner, he inevitably surrounded himself with the portentousness inseparable from the cultural atmosphere of those days, and in pursuit of his 'mission' entirely absorbed the lives and personalities of his wife and his friends. Yet it would be wrong to regard this as the whole picture.

Beneath all this, the man was very human. There was his strong sense of humour, his constant willingness to help other musicians, his final remorse and attempted atonement for having unwittingly starved his wife of love and affection. Above all, there was the fact that, like other 'great artists', he was not simply concerned with himself, but tormented by human problems in general. Bruno Walter describes how Mahler's expression would plunge suddenly from cheerfulness to gloom, and he would say: 'What grim darkness underlies life! Whence have we come? Whither are we bound? Is it true, as Schopenhauer says, that I willed this life before I was conceived? Why do I fancy I am free, when my character constricts me like a prison? To what purpose is all this toil and suffering? How can cruelty and evil be the work of a loving God? Will death at last reveal the meaning of life?' The equivalence of 'I' and 'we' shows clearly Mahler's sense of oneness with humanity, as his contrast of 'freedom' with 'constricting character' reveals him facing the crucial romantic (and human) dilemma. The true justification of Mahler the 'great artist' is that he did have something vital to say, and, like Wagner, devoted his whole existence to saying it.

What was it that he said? Mahler's inner conflict was the eternal one between innocence and experience, idealism and realism, affirmation and denial. Of a basically life-loving nature, he was confronted from the beginning with the problems of cruelty, pain and death, and thus with the question of the value and purpose of human life. He could not fall back trustingly on an inherited faith, like Bruckner; he could not accept either the Jewish religion (his own father was a free-thinker) or the official Austrian Catholic religion (though he did undergo baptism and struggled hard for faith, even achieved it at times). Nor could he ignore the question, like Strauss, nor give a firm negative answer and embrace hedonism, like Delius. The problem persistently tormented him, and his life and art became a quest for the truth.

He was one of those like Keats, for whom 'the miseries of the world are misery, and will not let them rest'. Or, to substitute his name for Webster's in T. S. Eliot's lines: 'Mahler was much possessed by death and saw the skull beneath the skin'. But the other side of the picture should be stressed. His obsession with suffering was the inverse product of an instinctive belief in life. Too much has been made of Mahler's 'self-pity' and 'pessimism', on the strength of his last works, written under the shadow of death. He was a healthy lover of life – a swimmer, a walker, a hill-climber; even after the doctor's death sentence he could say 'I am thirstier than ever for life'. And there is much exultant energy of spirit in his music: six of his eleven symphonic works reach out all-embracingly towards humanity, like Beethoven's. Many of his movements are full of the sheer joy of living; this even shines through the unutterable sadness of the valedictory finale of the Ninth Symphony, and springs up resurgent in the (unfinished) scherzo of the Tenth. Only because Mahler's instinctive, positive side was beset by 'the spirit that denies', did he become the quintessential voice of romantic discontent.

But there was more to it than romanticism. What affronts the idealist – the cruelty, vulgarity, triviality and apparent meaninglessness of life – he stared boldly in the face: he neither escaped from it into a private paradise like the late romantics, nor ignored it altogether as a non-artistic element like the classics, but acknowledged it and fought against it. This is the 'difference' that sets Mahler apart from the romantics, and indeed from all other composers. If half of him was a romantic, the other half was that characteristic twentieth-century figure: the restless seeker for the naked truth (whether 'beautiful' or 'ugly'), ridden with doubt and perplexity, ill-at-ease in an unfriendly cosmos.

*

Obviously, a man like Mahler would never achieve the Olympian calm of a Beethoven or the cool detachment of a Stravinsky; nor, on the other hand, the nihilism of an Alban Berg. In fact, there is no one like Mahler; he is a composer *sui generis*. To justify this statement requires special pleading – of the kind which once had to explain that Wagner's operas contained no arias and Hugo Wolf's songs no tunes.

Mahler chose for his musical medium the symphony – the 'pure' musical form – which naturally invites a straight comparison with Beethoven, Brahms, or Sibelius. But in fact no such comparison is possible. His symphonies are of a different kind – a kind of their own, which can only be judged on their own standards.

Let us begin by tracing his musical antecedents. His symphonies stem from the 'programme symphony' originated by Beethoven. Beethoven stood between two worlds, classic and romantic; and the romantics' view of him as pro-gramme-symphonist, derived from the Eroica, Fifth, Pastoral and 'Choral', was no less legitimate than the moderns' view of him as pure symphonist, derived from the Fourth, Seventh and Eighth. But in Beethoven's programme symphonies, so classical in form, the programme is largely implicit; it was Berlioz who inaugurated the romantic symphony with a detailed programme, which was followed by Liszt and others. From Beethoven then, but through Berlioz and Liszt, Mahler inherited his conception of the symphony as a work concretely expressive of aspects of human life.

But Beethoven's expressive symphonic style was also developed by Wagner, in the explicit world of music-drama; and in using this style to express the emotions of his dramatic characters, Wagner increased the expressive power of symphonic music to an unprecedented degree. Mahler adopted this new expressive power. He once said: 'Wagner appropriated the means of expres-sion of symphonic music; and now, in the same way, the symphonic composer . . . will avail himself of the expressive power gained for music by the achieve-ment of Wagner'. He also derived from Wagner (through Bruckner) his vast time-scale. Mahler's symphonies stand in relation to Mozart's as *The Ring* does to *Don Giovanni*: as Wagner expanded operatic form to express an all-embracing view of life, and as Beethoven expanded the classical symphony for the same purpose, so did Mahler expand the Beethoven symphony to express a whole world of feeling.

From Beethoven's Ninth, he inherited the idea of including a chorus and soloists in a symphony; from Beethoven's Pastoral and Berlioz's *Fantastique*, he derived the liberty to have five movements if necessary, instead of the usual four; from Wagner the freedom to expand the orchestra according to expres-sive need, and (partly through Bruckner) a preference for brass tone for power-ful affirmation. What he did not derive from Wagner was his orchestral style; only a few hints from Berlioz went to the creation of his fantastic and uniquely expressive instrumentation.

Mahler's symphonies, then, are vast ambitious works in the programmatic tradition. But the word 'programmatic' needs clarification. A programme may be purely inward-emotional, as in Beethoven's Eroica, or part inward-emotional part outward-factual, as in Beethoven's Pastoral and Berlioz's *Fantastique*. And the factual element is always an embarrassment; since music, which can so profoundly express human feeling, seems childish when trying to portray concrete actuality. Hence Berlioz advised against printing the 'story' of the *Fantastique* in concert programmes, desiring the work to stand on its musical (and, we may add, emotionally expressive) merits.

Likewise Tchaikovsky, providing a programme for his Fourth, to please Nadezhda von Meck, stressed the danger of expounding music in words, describing his attempt as 'chaotic and incomplete'.

Nevertheless, programmes were not just a game. The romantics intended their symphonies to be expressive of life; the difficulty was explaining in words just what they expressed. Thus Tchaikovsky, when Taneyev objected to the Fourth Symphony's programmatic nature, replied: 'I . . . don't see why you should consider that a defect. On the contrary I should be sorry if symphonies that meant nothing flowed from my pen. . . . Most assuredly my symphony has a programme, but one that cannot be expressed in words: the attempt would be ludicrous. But is not this proper to a symphony? Should not a symphony reveal those wordless urges that hide in the heart, asking earnestly for expression?'

The trouble is that words tend to produce concrete images, and these distract from the music's real purport, which is emotional or psychological. Hence Mahler, asked by a journalist for the 'meaning' of his Second Symphony, replied: 'I believe I have expressed my intention clearly enough in the music. When I conceived it, I was in no way concerned with a detailed programme of events, but at most with an emotion.' Yet he eventually gave the Second a programme – only to reject it later! But this is understandable: he wanted, he said, to leave the interpretation to the 'individual insight of the listener'; finding little insight, he tried to explain in words; finding the words taken literally instead of symbolically, he withdrew them.

This discussion of romantic musical 'meaning' may be summed up by the clear-headed Wagner. 'When the musician feels prompted to sketch the smallest composition, he owes it simply to the stimulus of a feeling that usurps his whole being at the hour of conception. This mood may be brought about by an outward experience, or have risen from a secret inner spring; whether it shows itself as melancholy, joy, desire, contentment, love or hatred, in the musician it will always take a musical shape. . . . But grand, passionate, lasting emotions, these drive the musician to those vaster, more intense conceptions to which we owe, among other things, the origin of a Sinfonia Eroica. These greater moods, such as deep suffering of soul or potent exultation, may date from outer causes . . . but when they force the musician to creation, they have already turned to music in him, so that at the moment of creative inspiration, it is no longer the outer event that governs the composer, but the musical sensation it has begotten in him. . . .'

The programmes of Mahler's symphonies, then, are largely interior ones, concerned with deep-seated emotions rather than with external actuality. Their overall form normally derives from Beethoven's Fifth and Tchaikovsky's Fourth: presentation of a conflict in the opening movement; descent to a more relaxed mood in the second; return to the plane of the first movement in the finale, which brings a resolution. But this form is considerably expanded: the first movement is larger and more discursive; the central two (or three, or four) are often extremely variegated – facets bearing on the main idea; the finale is usually vast and complex. In each symphony, this general pattern is refashioned according to expressive need, and sometimes subtilized into a new conception. The forms of the movements themselves are developments of traditional ones – sonata form, scherzo and trio (or trios), funeral march, variations, rondo; the slow movements, like Bruckner's, are normally modelled on the Adagio of Beethoven's Ninth – varied alternation of two themes, with a powerful culmination based on the first.

Mahler's form is widely regarded as his weakest point; but once his highly original expressive intention is understood – to unify a large number of con-flicting moods – his control over his gigantic schemes appears amazingly sure, often masterly. Clear lines can be drawn between total success (e.g. the whole of the Sixth), partial success (e.g. the finale of the Fifth), and partial failure (e.g. the opening movement of the Third), but only when his revolutionary methods have been fully grasped. Before condemning Mahler's formal methods out of hand, the listener should read Schoenberg's analysis, in *Style and Idea*, of the subtly-shaped main theme of the Andante of the Sixth Symphony, or himself analyse the opening theme of the scherzo of the Fifth, with its twelve-bar contraction of an implied sixteen-bar theme. And if he analyses a whole movement, he will usually discover mastery on the widest scale, with a close thematic coherence tautly unifying a mass of multifarious detail.

But even when Mahler temporarily loses grasp, the grandeur of the overall conception and the fascination of the material are sufficient to justify his claim to greatness. After all, it is only in music that a work is damned for be-ing imperfect; no one questions the immense stature of Dickens, for example, despite his enormous imperfections. Mahler's greatness resides in his endless supply of significant material, developed with great originality into forms which, perfect or imperfect, ultimately bear the weight of a large concep-tion.

Which brings us to the question of the value of his material. His adoption of many different styles to suit his expressive intention of 'building up a world of feeling' led early critics to declare that he had no style of his own at all. But he redeemed any borrowings by imprinting his personality vividly on practically every note. In any case, most of his material is the undeniable pro-duct of his own fantastic invention. To give a brief abstract of his style is impossible, since each of his works inhabits a world of its own; however, a summary of certain basic recurring elements can give an idea of it, and of some of the things he says in his symphonies. To begin with his positive, in-stinctive side – his delight in nature and life – there is the Austrian folk style, ingrained from childhood, and also derived through Schubert and Bruckner. Then there is the Faustian element, the yearning for fullness of being: an individual modification of Wagner's soaring melody and chromatic harmony. Next, discouragement, 'the spirit that denies', tormented despair, and the terror of death: here the quintessential Mahler appears, throwing grisly shadows across the music of life's joy, distorting it, disintegrating it with hideous chromaticisms and grotesque orchestration.

Then there is the struggle against fate. 'Fate' was a living reality to the romantics – 'I will take fate by the throat' said Beethoven – but it may need re-defining nowadays as the threat of destruction caused by the impingement of untoward external events on human weakness. Hammering rhythms are used, like those in Beethoven and Tchaikovsky, but more nervous; and a resolution of the struggle emerges. This may be reassertion of the validity of human effort, in pounding march rhythms; faith in God, in a noble chorale style derived from Bruckner; acceptance of death itself, either as defeat, in funeral-march rhythm, or as a haven of eternal peace, in the late romantic 'sunset' vein (in the last two works).

Above all, there is the astounding originality of the purely Mahlerian elements: the aforesaid 'distortion' music; the elemental voices of nature, mysterious and lonely, or brutally ferocious; the cosmic power of the funeral march; the sheer horror of some of the scherzos; the bounding ebullience of some of the Ländler; the exultant stride of the triumphal marches; the ecstatic outbursts of jubilation. These unique conceptions stamp Mahler as a highly original genius.

Much of their quality is due, of course, to the amazing orchestration; but this point needs slightly elucidating. Mahler, like Berlioz, Wagner, Sibelius and others, in no sense 'orchestrated' his music, but conceived it straightaway for orchestra. The significance of the material is inseparable from its instrumental form: to take only one example, the 'hollow' main material of the Ländler of the Ninth Symphony sounds like simple 'gay' music on the piano; its hollowness resides in its sardonic scoring, imagined with it from the outset. There is no point in trying to give an inventory of Mahler's orchestration, even if it were possible: it is his most admired feature, and it speaks for itself.

Another powerful expressive element in Mahler's music is his use of 'progressive tonality' – the procedure of resolving a symphonic conflict in a different key from that in which it was stated. He and Carl Nielsen inaugurated this procedure independently. Mussorgsky had used it on a small scale in the Serenade in the *Songs and Dances of Death* (1875), which moves from E minor to E flat minor. Mahler took it up in his early song 'Erinnerung' (*c.* 1883), moving from G minor to A minor, and first used it symphonically in his First Symphony (1888): the work is in D, but the finale opens in F minor and only after a long struggle breaks through into D. Nielsen first applied the process to a whole symphony – his No. 1 (1892) is a G minor work ending in C; Mahler followed independently in his Second Symphony (1894), which moves from C minor to E flat. Mahler most probably derived the idea from Wagner, who, after all, initiated the idea of moving from one tonal world to another over the course of a large-scale work: *The Rhinegold* (1854) and the whole *Ring* (1873) move from E flat to D flat; *Tristan* (1865) moves from A minor to B. Mahler's use of keys, like Wagner's, was primarily 'psychological'; nevertheless, he handled tonality, as did Wagner, with absolute technical mastery. Anyone who cares to analyse his large-scale tonal schemes within movements will find a complete creative control over this all-important element of symphonic construction.

❋

And now for Mahler's 'difference'. What bewilders many in his music is its frequent recourse to banal sounds from the outside world: bird-calls, bugle-fanfares, cheap popular music, military marches. These appear to be crude programmatic elements of the worst type – references to external actuality, making the music impure. In fact, Mahler's music *is* impure – but in a unique way, and intentionally so. In a letter to Bruno Walter concerning the Third Symphony, he said: 'I have no doubts that our friends the critics . . . will once again suffer from dizziness . . . the whole thing is . . . tainted with my deplorable sense of humour. . . . It is well known that I cannot do without trivialities. This time, however, all permissible bounds have been passed. "One often feels that one has got into a pub or a pig-sty!" ' This strange aspect of Mahler's style is the truly revolutionary element in his music, the essence of his genius, giving his works an extra perspective rarely glimpsed before or since.

It can best be explained by a literary analogy. Aldous Huxley, in an essay in the volume *Music at Night*, distinguishes between 'tragedy' and 'the Whole Truth'. He says: 'To make a tragedy the artist must isolate a single element out of the totality of human experience and use that exclusively as his material. Tragedy is something that is separated out from the Whole Truth, distilled from it . . . chemically pure. . . . It is because of its chemical purity that tragedy so effectively performs its function of catharsis. . . . From the reading or hearing of a tragedy, we rise with the feeling that

> Our friends are exultations, agonies,
> And love, and man's unconquerable mind;

and the heroic conviction that we too should be unconquerable if subjected to the agonies; that . . . we too should continue to love, might even learn to exult. . . .'

As an example of the Whole Truth, Huxley takes the scene in *Tom Jones* in which the idealized heroine Sophia Western falls from her horse on top of the fat innkeeper who is helping her off, to the amusement of the yokels: 'Fielding refused to impose the tragedian's veto; he shirked nothing – neither the intrusion of irrelevant absurdities into the midst of romance and disaster, nor any of life's no less irrelevantly painful interruptions of the course of happiness.' And he points out that 'in recent times literature has become more and more acutely conscious of the Whole Truth – of the great ocean of irrelevant things, events and thoughts stretching away endlessly in every direction. . . .'

15

Now symphonic music normally possesses the 'chemical purity' of tragedy: in Beethoven's Fifth, the composer's 'agonies and exultations' have been distilled into the patterns of classical music, and the irrelevancies of life excluded. It would be difficult to imagine how they could have been included, in the interests of the Whole Truth, had not Mahler shown the way. On the basic pattern of 'chemically pure' music, he superimposed the Whole Truth by bringing in 'irrelevant absurdities' from everyday life: sounds from nature and popular music. They are not programmatic elements in the crude sense; they do stand for their counterparts in the external world, admittedly, but only as symbols. Let us take an example, using another literary analogy.

T. S. Eliot ends his poem *Triumphal March* as follows:

> Now they go up to the temple. Then the sacrifice.
> Now come the virgins bearing urns, urns containing
> Dust
> Dust
> Dust of dust, and now
> Stone, bronze, stone, steel, stone, oakleaves, horses' heels
> Over the paving.

(This is the lofty plane of 'tragedy'; but now we turn to the crowd:)

> That is all we could see. But how many eagles! and how many trumpets!
> (And Easter Day, we didn't get to the country,
> So we took young Cyril to church. And they rang a bell
> And he said right out loud, *crumpets*.)
>   Don't throw away that sausage,
> It'll come in handy. He's artful. Please, will you
> Give us a light?
> Light
> Light
> *Et les soldats faisaient la haie? ILS LA FAISAIENT.*

This is 'impure' art — the Whole Truth. The descent into everyday banality, and the return to the tragic plane as the 'light' for a cigarette becomes the 'light' mankind has need of — these form a close literary parallel to Mahler's methods (even down to the quotation from someone else's work in a foreign language; though this obscure line need not concern us).

Compare the second movement of the Fifth Symphony. This is largely 'chemically pure' — a vehement lament enclosing symphonic funeral-march elements. The main 'grief' motive is an agonizing leap of a minor ninth falling to the octave; after much turmoil, the funeral-march section takes it up in nobly tragic fashion. But there is suddenly a 'tasteless' interruption: the motive whisks away in the major as a jaunty 'popular' march tune of the utmost triviality (cf. 'Please will you give us a light?'). However, this march works swiftly, changing character, to a violent climax, and Mahler then hurls out the motive exultantly on the trumpets; later it becomes a majestic chorale (cf.

'Light Light'). Again, Mahler's funereal canon on 'Frère Jacques' in the First
Symphony might be compared to Eliot's 'Here we go round the prickly pear'.

For Mahler, music had to include the trivialities and absurdities of everyday life, for only after facing these petty but powerful enemies could he wring
victory out of tragedy, or, at worst, go down in genuinely tragic defeat. Consequently, his triumph in the Fifth Symphony is utterly different from the
'chemically pure' triumph in the finale of Beethoven's Fifth. But as Huxley says:
'There is no reason, after all, why the Chemically Impure and the Chemically
Pure, the Whole Truth and the Partial Truth, should not exist simultaneously,
each in its separate sphere. The human spirit has need of both.'

Mahler's attempt to make music take in the whole of life was a bold ven-
ture. It was psychologically conditioned, as Donald Mitchell has made clear.
Late in life Mahler, worried about his marital relationship, had an interview
with Freud, and one childhood memory, among others, came to light: during
a 'specially painful scene' between his father and mother, he had rushed into
the street to find a hurdy-gurdy grinding out the popular Viennese tune 'O du
lieber Augustin'. He declared that the conjunction of high tragedy and light
amusement was from then on inextricably fixed in his mind, and the one
mood brought the other with it. No doubt. But this psychological cause only
led him to a universal truth realized by Shakespeare when he put the Fool in
King Lear: there is no more effective way of highlighting tragedy than to bring
the trivial and ribald into grotesque opposition with it.

But is it justifiable in music? Mahler had a few precedents. There is the
'popular' wind-band in the finale of Beethoven's 'Choral' Symphony, which, as
Robert Simpson says, seems suddenly to reveal man as something small and
insignificant, until the jaunty march tune is developed as a driving symphonic
allegro, restoring him to the heroic plane. Again, the trumpets and drums of
war intrude into the 'dona nobis pacem' of the *Missa Solemnis*. Berlioz was
another forerunner in the 'March to the Scaffold' with his vision of the mob –
a 'popular' military band luridly setting off the grim procession of death; and
in the 'Witches' Sabbath', with his sadistic transmogrification of 'the beloved'
into a witch – the graceful *idée fixe* cackling away on the shrilly vulgar E flat
clarinet in an ungainly jig rhythm.

Since Mahler there have been other examples; the 'cheap' dance music in
Berg's *Wozzeck* and Britten's *Peter Grimes*, the side-drum of war in Nielsen's
Fifth, the tenor saxophone's 'swing music' in Vaughan Williams's Sixth. With
these distinguished examples in mind, we should think very hard before condemning Mahler's 'banalities' out of hand. Modern music has moved in the
opposite direction from Mahler – away from life towards 'pure art'; but only
if we can admit the validity of the romantic view of music as emotional expression, and Mahler's own view of music as emotional expression plus the
Whole Truth, shall we see the full significance of his art.

Any assessment of it as 'pure music' by Beethovenian standards is meaningless: if Beethoven's symphonies are like perfect poetic odes or taut classical

dramas, Mahler's are like roomy, discursive volumes of autobiography. But though they are 'impure', they are none the less essentially on the tragic plane. Huxley's summing-up is entirely applicable to Mahler: 'In Wholly-Truthful art, the agonies may be just as real, love and the unconquerable mind just as important as in tragedy . . . but the agonies and indomitabilities are placed by the Wholly-Truthful writer in another, wider context.'

THE MUSIC

EARLY WORKS

Juvenilia. Most of Mahler's youthful music was either destroyed or lost. All that apparently survives, apart from fragmentary sketches, is the complete opening movement of a Piano Quartet in A minor, probably dating from 1877 (first known performance in New York in 1964), and three complete songs with piano (1880) – 'Im Lenz', 'Winterlied' and 'Maitanz im Grünen' (all to poems by Mahler) which remain in private hands. ('Maitanz im Grünen' is virtually identical to 'Hans und Grete' from Volume I of the *Lieder und Gesänge*.) Donald Mitchell gives an account of these works in his book *Gustav Mahler: The Early Years*.

Das klagende Lied (The Song of Lament), *cantata for soprano, contralto, tenor, chorus and orchestra, completed in 1880, at the age of twenty.*

The text is Mahler's own, inspired by a fairy-tale by Ludwig Bechstein, based on an old German legend. Two brothers are both in love with the same proud and beautiful queen, and when the elder of the two knights comes across the younger one in a forest, he murders him as he lies sleeping peacefully there. But a wandering minstrel finds one of the boy's bones and fashions a flute from it, and when he plays this flute the boy's voice speaks through it, telling how he was murdered, and bidding the minstrel seek the castle where the elder brother is about to marry the queen. The minstrel arrives at the castle, and when the flute is played, the younger brother's voice rings out again, revealing to the queen and the assembled company the treachery of the bridegroom. The castle crumbles to dust, the queen sinks to the ground, and the wedding guests flee in terror.

21

The original version was in three parts – the forest legend (i.e. the murder), the minstrel, the wedding. In 1893 Mahler discarded the first part and revised the remainder, conducting the first performance in Vienna in 1901. Which suggests that the published version is no early work, but a mature re-composition – quite wrongly: in essentials the original is unchanged. Already, Mahler's individual orchestral style was formed; in the revision, he merely made the texture and scoring even more effective. As composer, too, he had already, as he said, 'found himself as Mahler'; when revising he tidied up details, but left the shape of the work unchanged.

The cantata shows his early mastery of the post-Wagnerian apparatus, and his strong sense of key-psychology: tragic C minor, pastoral F major, festive C major, and final desolate A minor. The orchestral introduction* reveals his characteristic large time-scale, predilection for march rhythms, deep feeling for nature, and sense of Germanic fairy-tale *grotesquerie*. The initial bass motive, with its tonic-dominant fourths, is *echt* Mahler, as are the naked contrapuntal lines of the woodwind; the whole closely foreshadows the opening of the Second Symphony. If the early climax is undigested Bruckner, the F major horn calls, contradicting C minor, are pure Mahler, as is the profusion of clearly related motives; the 'Dies Irae' brass chorale again foreshadows the Second Symphony. The minstrel's carefree tune anticipates Mahler's folk-vein; the intricate woodwind meanderings shortly afterwards are prophetic of *The Song of the Earth*; after the opening narration, the timpani's tramping fourths are a Mahlerian fingerprint. Entirely characteristic is the bone-flute's song (contralto – 'Ach Spielmann'), with its Slav folk-style and rapid key-switches a tone higher; so is the final clinching of the structure by a return of the introduction's climax, reinforced by the chorus.

Part 11's opening festal music recalls early Wagner, but the 'popular' off-stage band, and later the distortion of the festal music by muted brass, are prophetic. The contralto solo 'Was ist der König?' and the minstrel's arrival, bringing back themes from Part 1, show Mahler's large-scale formal methods (cf. Symphony 8). The Mahlerian Whole Truth appears for the first time with the intrusion of the 'trivial' off-stage music into the tragic choral outburst: further portents are the final choral lament, anticipating the finale of the First Symphony; the bare string counterpoints when the tenor describes the final desolation; the shadowy disintegration of the texture.

The cantata, delightful despite weaknesses, was a false start: Mahler was to be a symphonist, not a musical story-teller. Nevertheless, certain passionate exclamations written on the manuscript against the passage telling of the younger brother's death (memories of Ernst?) show already his close identification of music with life.

---

* i.e. to Part 1 of the revised version, entitled *Der Spielmann* in the original version. Similarly 'Part 11' here refers to the original version's *Hochzeitsstück*. [D.M.]

WALDMÄRCHEN

Es war eine stolze Königin
Gar lieblich ohne Massen;
Kein Ritter stand nach ihrem Sinn,
Sie wollt' sie alle hassen.
O weh! Du wonnigliches Weib!
Wem blühet wohl dein süsser Leib?

Im Wald eine rote Blume stand,
Ach, so schön wie die Königinne;
Welch Rittersmann die Blume fand,
Der konnt' die Frau gewinnen!
O weh! Du stolze Königin!
Wann bricht er wohl, dein stolzer Sinn?

Zwei Brüder zogen zum Walde hin,
Sie wollten die Blume suchen;
Der Eine hold und von mildem Sinn,
Der And're konnte nur fluchen!
O Ritter, schlimmer Ritter mein,
O liessest du das Fluchen sein!

Als sie so zogen eine Weil',
Da kamen sie zu scheiden;
Das war ein Suchen nun im Eil'
Im Wald und auf der Heiden!
Ihr Ritter mein, im schnellen Lauf,
Wer findet wohl die Blume?

Der Junge zieht durch Wald und Heid',
Er braucht nicht lang zu geh'n;
Bald sieht er von ferne bei der Weid'
Die rote Blume steh'n.
Die hat er auf den Hut gesteckt,
Und dann zur Ruhe sich hingestreckt.

Der And're zieht im wilden Hang,
Umsonst durchsucht er die Heide,
Und als der Abend hernieder sank,
Da kommt er zur grünen Weide!
O weh! Wem er dort schlafend fand,
Die Blume am Hut, am grünen Band!

Du wonnigliche Nachtigall,
Und Rotkehlchen hinter der Hecken,
Wollt ihr mit eurem süssen Schall
Den armen Ritter erwecken?

FOREST LEGEND

There once was a proud queen,
Lovely beyond measure;
No knight could win her favour,
She looked with scorn on all.
O woe, wondrous lady!
For whom will your love bloom?

In the forest grew a red flower,
O, as fair as the queen;
The knight who found the flower
Would win her for his wife.
O woe, proud queen!
When will your proud spirit be broken?

Two brothers went into the forest
In search of the flower;
One was kind and gentle,
The other could only blaspheme.
O knight, evil knight,
Give up your blasphemy!

When they had gone a little while,
They parted from each other;
And now each of them hastened
To search both wood and heath.
You knights, in such a hurry,
Which of you will find the flower?

The younger went through wood and heath,
He did not need to search for long;
Soon he saw, from afar, by a willow,
The red flower growing.
He fixed it to his cap,
And then lay down to rest.

The other roamed a wild ravine,
He searched the heath in vain,
And as evening drew on,
He came to the green willow.
O woe to him he found sleeping there,
The flower in his cap, tied with green.

You, wondrous nightingale,
And robin of the hedgerows,
Won't you waken the poor knight
With your sweet song?

Du rote Blume hinter'm Hut,	*You, red flower in his cap,*
Du blinkst und glänzest ja wie Blut!	*You gleam and glint like blood!*

Ein Auge blickt in wilder Freud',	*An eye gleams in wild joy,*
Dess' Schein hat nicht gelogen;	*Its semblance does not lie;*
Ein Schwert von Stahl glänzt ihm zur Seit',	*A steel sword glints at his side,*
Das hat er nun gezogen.	*And now he has drawn it.*
Der Alte lacht unter'm Weidenbaum,	*The elder laughs under the willow tree,*
Der Junge lächelt wie im Traum.	*The younger smiles as if dreaming.*

Ihr Blumen, was seid ihr vom Tau so schwer?	*Flowers, why are you so heavy with dew?*
Mir scheint, das sind gar Tränen!	*They look like tears to me.*
Ihr Winde, was weht ihr so traurig daher,	*Breezes, why do you blow so sadly thence,*
Was will euer Raunen und Wähnen?	*What does your whispering mean?*
"Im Wald, auf der grünen Heide,	*'In the forest, on the green heath,*
Da steht eine alte Weide."	*There stands an old willow.'*

DER SPIELMANN / THE MINSTREL

Beim Weidenbaum, im kühlen Tann,	*By a willow tree, in a cool forest,*
Da flattern die Dohlen und Raben,	*Where jackdaws and ravens hover,*
Da liegt ein blonder Rittersmann	*There lies a fair-headed knight*
Unter Blättern und Blüten begraben.	*Buried under leaves and blossoms.*
Dort ist's so lind und voll von Duft,	*It is so calm and fragrant there,*
Als ging ein Weinen durch die Luft!	*As if weeping filled the air.*
O Leide, Leide!	*O sorrow, sorrow!*

Ein Spielmann zog einst des Weges daher,	*A minstrel once went that way,*
Da sah er ein Knöchlein blitzen;	*He saw a bone gleaming there;*
Er hob es auf, als wär's ein Rohr,	*He picked it up, as if it were a reed*
Wollt' sich eine Flöte d'raus schnitzen.	*From which he might cut a flute.*
O Spielmann, lieber Spielmann mein,	*O minstrel, dear minstrel mine,*
Das wird ein seltsam Spielen sein!	*It will be strange music that you play.*
O Leide, weh! O Leide!	*O sorrow, woe, sorrow!*

Der Spielmann setzt die Flöte an,	*The minstrel put the flute to his mouth*
Und lässt sie laut erklingen:	*And let it play loudly.*
O Wunder, was nun da begann!	*O wonder, at what now began,*
Welch' seltsam traurig Singen!	*What strange and mournful singing!*
Es klingt so traurig und doch so schön!	*So mournful and yet so beautiful,*
Wer's hört, der möcht' vor Leid vergeh'n!	*Whoever heard it might die of sorrow.*
O Leide, Leide!	*O sorrow, sorrow!*

"Ach Spielmann, lieber Spielmann mein!	*'O minstrel, dear minstrel mine,*
Das muss ich dir nun klagen:	*I must tell you my grievous tale:*
Um ein schönfarbig Blümelein	*For a brightly coloured flower*

Hat mich mein Bruder erschlagen!	*My brother murdered me.*
Im Walde bleicht mein junger Leib!	*My young bones bleach in the forest,*
Mein Bruder freit ein wonnig Weib!	*My brother woos a fair bride.*
O Leide, Leide! Weh! "	*O sorrow, sorrow, woe!'*

Der Spielmann ziehet in die Weit',	*The minstrel went far and wide,*
Lässt's überall erklingen.	*Everywhere playing his music.*
"Ach weh, ach weh, ihr lieben Leut'!	*'Alas, alas, dear people,*
Was soll denn euch mein Singen?	*What do you think of my song?*
Hinauf muss ich zu des Königs Saal!	*I must go to the royal castle,*
Hinauf! zu des Königs holdem Gemahl!"	*To the king's fair bride.'*
O Leide, weh! O Leide!	*O sorrow, woe, sorrow!*

HOCHZEITSSTÜCK   WEDDING PIECE

Vom hohen Felsen erglänzt das Schloss.	*The castle gleams from a high crag,*
Die Zinken erschall'n und Drometten.	*Trumpets and cornets resound;*
Dort sitzt der mutigen Ritter Tross,	*There sits the band of brave knights,*
Die Frau'n mit goldenen Ketten.	*And their ladies with gold necklaces.*
Was will Wohl der jubelnde, fröhliche Schall?	*What does this joyful, festive sound mean?*
Was leuchtet und glänzt im Königssaal?	*What glitters and shines in the great hall?*
O Freude, heia! Freude!	*Joy, O joy!*

Und weisst du's nicht, warum die Freud'?	*And do you not know the reason for this joy?*
Hei! dass ich dir's sagen kann!	*Indeed, I can tell you:*
Die Königin hält Hochzeit heut'!	*The queen is to be married today*
Mit dem jungen Rittersmann!	*To the young knight.*
Seht hin! die stolze Königin!	*See there, the proud queen!*
Heut' bricht er doch, ihr stolzer Sinn!	*Today her proud spirit shall be broken.*
O Freude, heia! Freude!	*Joy, O joy!*

Was ist der König so stumm und bleich?	*Why is the king so numb and pale?*
Hört nicht des Jubels Töne!	*He does not hear the joyful sounds,*
Sieht nicht die Gäste, stolz und reich,	*He does not see the guests, so proud and rich,*
Sieht nicht der Königin holde Schöne!	*Or the queen's ravishing beauty.*
Was ist der König so bleich und stumm?	*Why is the king so pale and silent?*
Was geht ihm wohl im Kopf herum?	*What disturbs his peace of mind?*
Ein Spielmann tritt zur Türe herein,	*A minstrel comes to the door.*
Was mag's wohl mit dem Spielmann sein?	*What has the minstrel come for?*
O Leide, Leide! Weh!	*O sorrow, sorrow, woe!*

"Ach Spielmann, lieber Spielmann mein!	*'O minstrel, dear minstrel mine,*
Das muss ich dir nun klagen!	*Now I must tell you my grievous tale:*
Um ein schönfarbig Blümelein	*For a brightly coloured flower*
Hat mich mein Bruder erschlagen!	*My brother murdered me.*
Im Walde bleicht mein junger Leib,	*My young bones bleach in the forest,*
Mein Bruder freit ein wonnig Weib!"	*My brother woos a fair bride.'*
O Leide, weh, O Leide!	*O sorrow, woe, sorrow!*

B

Auf springt der König von seinem Thron!
Und blickt auf die Hochzeitsrund!
Und nimmt die Flöte in frevelndem Hohn
Und setzt sie selbst an den Mund!
O Schrecken, was nun da erklang!
Hört ihr die Märe, todesbang!

"Ach Bruder, lieber Bruder mein!
Du hast mich ja erschlagen!
Nun bläst du auf meinem Totenbein!
Dess' muss ich ewig klagen!
Was hast du mein junges Leben,
Dem Tode hingegeben?"
O Leide, weh, O Leide!

Am Boden liegt die Königin!
Die Pauken verstummem und Zinken.
Mit Schrecken die Ritter und Frauen flieh'n.
Die alten Mauern sinken!
Die Lichter verloschen im Königssaal.
Was ist es wohl mit dem Hochzeitsmahl?
Ach Leide!

The king leaps up from his throne
And looks at his wedding guests;
He takes the flute contemptuously
And puts it to his mouth.
O horror, what sounds forth now!
Do you hear the frightening story?

'O brother, dear brother mine,
It was you who murdered me;
Now that you play on my bone,
I must for ever accuse you.
Why have you given to Death
My young life?'
O sorrow, woe, sorrow!

The queen sinks to the ground,
Trumpets and drums are silent;
The knights and their ladies flee in terror,
The ancient ramparts crumble.
The lights have gone out in the great hall.
What is left now of the wedding feast?
O sorrow!

FIRST PERIOD

Adopting the useful three-period division, Mahler's first period comprises Symphonies 1–4 and various sets of songs; the latter are partly germinal to the symphonies.

LIEDER UND GESÄNGE (VOL. 1), *five songs with piano (1880–7?).*
Only three are of real interest. The charming 'Frühlingsmorgen', stemming from Schumann, and the haunting 'Erinnerung', more purely Mahlerian in its aching chromatic passion, represent another false start, being Lieder; Mahler was to find his original voice in a symphonic revitalization of the popular folk tradition – as is shown in 'Hans und Grete', a straight Ländler with words and music by Mahler himself. Here, in the crudest possible form, we find the *keck* (cheeky) popular vein which will permeate the symphonies, together with the 'symphonic' accompaniment based on short motives capable of development. Actually, the start was not false, for 'Hans und Grete' came before the two Lieder; composed in 1880, it was the first song Mahler cared to preserve.

Lieder und Gesänge, Volume 1

FRÜHLINGSMORGEN	SPRING MORNING
Es klopft an das Fenster der Lindenbaum mit Zweigen, blütenbehangen:	*The linden tree is tapping on the window with its blossom-covered twigs:*
Steh' auf! Steh' auf! Was liegst du im Traum?	*Get up! Get up! Why do you lie dreaming?*
Die Sonn' ist aufgegangen!	*The sun has risen.*

Die Lerche ist wach, die Büsche weh'n!
Die Bienen summen und Käfer!
Und dein munteres Lieb hab' ich auch schon
    geseh'n.
Steh' auf, Langschläfer!

(R. Leander)

The lark's awake, the bushes stir in the
    breeze,
the bees and beetles are buzzing,
and I've already seen your lively
    sweetheart –
get up, sleepyhead!

ERINNERUNG

Es wecket meine Liebe
die Lieder immer wieder!
Es wecken meine Lieder
die Liebe immer wieder!

Die Lippen, die da träumen
von deinen heissen Küssen,
in Sang und Liedesweisen
von dir sie tönen müssen!

Und wollen die Gedanken
der Liebe sich entschlagen,
So kommen meine Lieder
zu mir mit Liebesklagen!

So halten mich in Banden
die Beiden immer wieder!
Es weckt das Lied die Liebe!
Die Liebe weckt die Lieder!

(R. Leander)

REMEMBERING

Again and again my love inspires songs,
again and again my songs inspire love.

The lips that dream of your ardent kisses
respond to you with songs and melodies.

And when my thoughts try to evade love,
my songs return, lamenting love.

So both in turn hold me captive, again and
    again:
The songs inspire love, love inspires the
    songs!

HANS UND GRETE

Ringel, ringel Reih'n!

Wer fröhlich ist, der schlinge sich ein!
Wer Sorgen hat, der lass' sie daheim!
Wer ein liebes Liebchen küsst, wie glücklich
    der ist!

Ei, Hänschen, du hast ja kein's!
So suche dir ein's!
Ein liebes Liebchen, das ist was Fein's.
Juchhe! Juchhe!

HANS AND GRETE

Ring-a-ring o' roses!

If you're happy, join in the dance,
if you've got worries, leave them at home,
if you kiss your sweetheart, how lucky you
    are!

Hey, Hansi, you haven't got one –
so look for one!
A loving sweetheart, that's the thing!
Hurrah! Hurrah!

28

Ringel, ringel, Reih'n!

Ei, Gretchen, was stehst denn so allein?
Guckst doch hinüber zum Hänselein! ?

Und ist doch der Mai so grün! ?
Und die Lüfte, sie zieh'n!

Ei seht doch den dummen Hans!
Wie er rennet zum Tanz!
Er suchte ein Liebchen, Juchhe! Er fand's!

Ringel, ringel Reih'n!

    (*Mahler*)

Ring-a-ring o' roses!

Hey, Gretel, why standing alone?
But peeping at Hansi over there?

And isn't the month of May so green?
And the air is so sweet!

Hey now, look at stupid Hans,
how he runs to the dance!
He looked for a sweetheart – hurrah!
   – and he found one!

Ring-a-ring o' roses!

SERENADE *aus* DON JUAN

(*mit Begleitung von Blasinstrumenten*)

Ist's dein Wille, süsse Maid,
meinem heissen Liebesstreben
erst im Tode Raum zu geben,
o, da wart' ich lange Zeit!

Soll ich deine Gunst geniessen
erst nach meinem Erdengange,
währt mein Leben allzulange!
Mag es gleich im Nu zerfliessen!

Ist's dein Wille, süsse, Maid,
meinem heissen Liebesstreben
erst im Tode Raum zu geben,
o das ist gar lange Zeit!

    (*Tirso de Molina*)

SERENADE *from* DON JUAN

(accompanied by wind instruments)

If it is your wish, sweet maiden, only to
yield to my ardent courting
in death, well – I shall have to
wait a long time.

If I am to enjoy your favours only after
I've left this earth, my life would be
too long – it might as well melt away at
once.

If it is your wish, sweet maiden, only to
yield to my ardent courting
in death, well – that's an awfully long time!

PHANTASIE *aus* DON JUAN

Das Mägdlein trat aus dem Fischerhaus,
die Netze warf sie in's Meer hinaus!

Und wenn kein Fisch in das Netz ihr ging,
die Fischerin doch die Herzen fing!

Die Winde streifen so kühl umher,
erzählen leis' eine alte Mär'!

FANTASY *from* DON JUAN

The girl, stepping out of the fishing hut,
casts her nets into the sea.

And even if she caught no fish,
the fisher-maid trapped hearts!

The winds so coolly caressing
whisper an old fairy-tale.

Die See erglühet im Abendrot,
die Fischerin fühlt nicht Liebesnot
  im Herzen!

(*Tirso de Molina/Mahler*)

The sea glows with the light of the setting sun,
but the fisher-maid's heart reflects no love!

LIEDER EINES FAHRENDEN GESELLEN (SONGS OF A WAYFARING LAD), *a cycle of four orchestral songs, composed 1883?–5; orchestrated 1893?.*

This is Mahler's first mature composition – a short 'Spring Journey' as opposed to Schubert's long 'Winter Journey'; the text is his own, in folk style.

It was with this early work, completed in his mid-twenties, that Mahler established the form of the orchestral song-cycle, of which he was to become the supreme exponent. Berlioz had composed his *Nuits d'été* as songs with piano, and only orchestrated them afterwards; the accompaniments of Wagner's *Wesendonk-Lieder* were also written for piano, and although two of them were conceived as sketches for *Tristan*, the orchestration of all but one of them was carried out by another hand. But the *Lieder eines fahrenden Gesellen*, though likewise composed originally with piano, were clearly conceived from the outset with the orchestra in mind; and Mahler's actual orchestration of them was merely a definitive presentation of them in their authentic form. (In fact Mahler called the original piano version a 'piano-reduction'.)

The music is mainly folk-derived, the orchestral part latently symphonic, the instrumentation fully fledged: a full orchestra is used, for extreme clarity rather than weight. Progressive tonality is employed throughout. No. 1 (D minor to G minor) contrasts the rejected lover's grief (Slav folk-style) with his delight in nature (a pastoral middle section with bird calls). In No. 2 (D to F sharp), the lover, setting off on a bright spring morning, finds consolation in natural beauty, but soon loses heart: an Austrian-type 'walking tune' gradually fades out into wistful romantic harmonies. No. 3 (D minor to E minor) tells of the 'red-hot knife' in the lover's breast: here the demonic Mahler makes his first appearance – fast tortured music, entirely unfolklike, with stuttering muted trumpets and menacing *sforzato* trombones. Thoughts of the beloved (shimmering strings, soft horn calls) generate a despairing *fortissimo* climax, which disintegrates the texture into shadowy mutterings. No. 4 (E minor to F minor) is the lover's last journey; unlike Schubert's protagonist, he finds lasting peace beneath his linden tree. Mahler's funeral-march style appears here, in muted tones, merging into an Austrian folk vein saddened by gentle chromaticisms.

Already we see the conflict to be worked out in the symphonies – love of nature and life combating emptiness and despair. The resolution this time is the youthful romantic illusion of 'death the comforter'.

I

Wenn mein Schatz Hochzeit macht,
fröhliche Hochzeit macht,
hab' ich meinen traurigen Tag!
Geh' ich in mein Kämmerlein,
dunkles Kämmerlein!
Weine! wein'! Um meinen Schatz,
um meinen lieben Schatz!

When my love becomes a bride,
becomes a happy bride,
that will be my saddest day.
I'll go into my little room,
gloomy little room,
weeping, weeping for my love,
for my dear love.

Blümlein blau! Blümlein blau!
Verdorre nicht, verdorre nicht!
Vöglein süss! Vöglein süss!
Du singst auf grüner Heide!
"Ach! wie ist die Welt so schön!
Ziküth! Ziküth!"

Floweret blue, floweret blue,
do not fade, do not fade!
Fledgling sweet, fledgling sweet,
you sing in the green meadow:
'Ah, how lovely is the world!
Jug-jug! Jug-jug!'

Singet nicht! Blühet nicht!
Lenz ist ja vorbei!
Alles Singen ist nun aus!
Des Abends, wenn ich schlafen geh',
denk' ich an mein Leide!
An mein Leide!

Do not sing, do not bloom;
spring is dead and gone.
Singing's done for ever now.
At evening, when I go to sleep,
I'll think upon my sorrow,
upon my sorrow.

II

Ging heut' Morgen über's Feld,
Tau noch auf den Gräsern hing,
sprach zu mir der lust'ge Fink:
"Ei, du! Gelt?
Guten Morgen! Ei, Gelt? Du!
Wird's nicht eine schöne Welt?
Zink! Zink! Schön und flink!
Wie mir doch die Welt gefällt!"

I went this morning through the fields,
dew still hung upon the grass,
spoke to me the merry finch:
'You there, hey –
good morning! Hey there, you –
won't it be a lovely day?
Tweet! Tweet! Fine and bright!
O but how I love the world!'

Auch die Glockenblum' am Feld
hat mir lustig, guter Ding',
mit den Glöckchen, klinge, kling,
ihren Morgengruss geschellt:
"Wird's nicht eine schöne Welt?
Kling! Kling! Schönes Ding!
Wie mir doch die Welt gefällt!
Heia!"

And the harebells in the field
told me merry, cheerful things,
with their bells, a-ting-a-ling,
rang their morning greeting out:
'Won't it be a lovely day?
Ting! Ting! Lovely thing!
O but how I love the world!
Hola!'

Und da fing im Sonnenschein
gleich die Welt zu funkeln an;
Alles, Alles, Ton und Farbe gewann!

Then began, in the sunshine,
all the world to glitter bright;
all things woke to colour and sound

31

Im Sonnenschein!	*in the sunshine,*
Blum' und Vogel, gross und klein!	*flower and bird, both great and small.*
"Guten Tag! Guten Tag!	*'Good day! Good day!*
Ist's nicht eine schöne Welt?	*Isn't it a lovely day?*
Ei, du! Gelt? Schöne Welt! "	*You there, hey — lovely day!'*
Nun fängt auch mein Glück wohl an?	*Will my joy now flower too?*
Nein! Nein! Das ich mein',	*No, no; well I know*
mir nimmer, nimmer blühen kann!	*'twill never, never bloom again.*

III

Ich hab' ein glühend Messer,	*I have a red-hot knife,*
ein Messer in meiner Brust,	*a knife in my breast.*
O weh! O weh!	*Woe's me! Woe's me!*
Das schneid't so tief	*It cuts so deep*
in jede Freud' und jede Lust,	*into every joy and every bliss,*
so tief! so tief!	*so deep! so deep!*
Es schneid't so weh und tief!	*It cuts so sharp and deep!*
Ach, was ist das für ein böser Gast!	*Ah what a cruel guest is this!*
Nimmer hält er Ruh',	*Never grants me peace,*
nimmer hält er Rast!	*never grants me rest!*
Nicht bei Tag,	*Not by day,*
nicht bei Nacht, wenn ich schlief!	*not by night, when I'd sleep.*
O weh! O weh! O weh!	*Woe's me! Woe's me! Woe's me!*
Wenn ich in den Himmel seh',	*When I look into the sky,*
seh' ich zwei blaue Augen steh'n!	*two eyes of blue look back at me.*
O weh! O weh!	*Woe's me! Woe's me!*
Wenn ich im gelben Felde geh',	*When through the yellow corn I go,*
seh' ich von fern das blonde Haar	*I see afar her golden hair*
im Winde weh'n! O weh! O weh!	*swept by the wind. Woe's me! Woe's me!*
Wenn ich aus dem Traum auffahr'	*When I start up out of dreams,*
und höre klingen ihr silbern Lachen,	*and hear the ring of her silvery laughter,*
O weh! O weh!	*woe's me! Woe's me!*
Ich wollt' ich läg' auf der schwarzen Bahr',	*I would that I lay on the black bier,*
könnt' nimmer, nimmer die Augen aufmachen!	*and could never more open my eyes!*

IV

Die zwei blauen Augen von meinem Schatz,	*The two blue eyes of my love,*
	they've sent me out into the wide world.

die haben mich in die weite Welt geschickt.	*So I had to take my leave*
Da musst' ich Abschied nehmen vom allerliebsten Platz!	*of the town so dear to me!*
O Augen blau, warum habt ihr mich angeblickt?	*O blue eyes, why did you look at me?*
Nun hab' ich ewig Leid und Grämen!	*Now I am full of grief and sorrow.*

die haben mich in die weite Welt
geschickt.
Da musst' ich Abschied nehmen
vom allerliebsten Platz!
O Augen blau, warum habt ihr mich
angeblickt?
Nun hab' ich ewig Leid und Grämen!

So I had to take my leave
of the town so dear to me!
O blue eyes, why did you look at me?
Now I am full of grief and sorrow.

Ich bin ausgegangen in stiller Nacht,
wohl über die dunkle Heide.
Hat mir niemand Ade gesagt, Ade!
Mein Gesell' war Lieb' und Leide!

I went out at the dead of night,
across the gloomy heath;
no-one said goodbye to me.
My companions were love and sorrow!

Auf der Strasse stand ein Lindenbaum,
da hab' ich zum ersten Mal im Schlaf
geruht!
Unter dem Lindenbaum,
Der hat seine Blüten über mich geschneit,
da wusst' ich nicht, wie das Leben tut,
war alles, alles wieder gut!
Ach, alles wieder gut!
Alles! Alles!
Lieb' und Leid, und Welt und Traum!

By the wayside stands a linden-tree;
and there at last I've found some sleep,
under the linden-tree.
It snowed its blossoms over me,
I knew no more of the evils of life,
for all things turned to good again,
O all to good again!
Everything, everything,
love, and grief, the world, my dreams!

SYMPHONY NO. 1 IN D (1885–8); *first performed in Budapest, 1889, under Mahler.*

The original title (*Titan*), from a novel by Jean Paul, and the programme (also loosely based on Jean Paul) were later withdrawn; the novel, in fact, merely mirrored Mahler's own inner conflict. George Brandes describes its 'titan' hero, Roquairol, as 'a prototype of the form in which the age moulded its passion and its despair . . . burning, conscious desire which develops into fantastic eccentricity, because circumstances have no use for it, and because it does not possess the power to take hold of reality, re-mould it and subject it to itself; it becomes a disease, which strikes inward and leads to morbid self-contemplation and suicide'. The youthful, romantic Mahler naturally identified himself with this character; but the symphony actually opens his own spiritual autobiography.

The orchestra is large: four flutes, oboes and clarinets, seven horns, four trumpets, and two timpanists. It would seem that Mahler began as he intended to continue; but in fact the only surviving MS of the symphony (dated 1893) uses the normal romantic orchestra of triple woodwind, four horns, three trumpets and three trombones: the revision for larger orchestra was not published until 1899. In this, Mahler not only expanded the orchestration, but also improved it: for example, the fanfare for clarinets at the start of the symphony is for horns in the MS, and the third movement's opening double-bass solo is doubled by solo cello.

More surprising is that the 1893 MS has *five* movements – after the present first movement comes a short C major piece entitled 'Blumine'. And here Mahler did begin as he intended to continue: only three of the later symphonies have the orthodox quota of four movements.

It has been suggested, though without foundation, that his publisher persuaded Mahler to eliminate 'Blumine' from the published score, against his inclination; and some musicians have advocated restoring it. But this is unthinkable, fascinating as it may be to hear the original five-movement version with its original orchestration. Mahler himself conducted later performances from the published score, and had he really wanted 'Blumine' restored, he would surely have left some authoritative statement to that effect. His initial reluctance to discard it was probably a desire to preserve a favourite piece from oblivion: as Donald Mitchell has shown, it was originally part of Mahler's successful incidental music for Scheffel's *Der Trompeter von Säkkingen*. Although its C major tonality is explicable as an early example of his unorthodox key-switches between movements, it cannot belong, since it ignores the other movements' preoccupation with the interval of the perfect fourth. Of particular interest is the original version's programme. Mahler called it, not a symphony, but a 'symphonic poem in two parts'. Part I, *Days of Youth – Flowers, Fruit and Thorns,* consisted of the first three movements: 1. *Spring without End,* the introduction representing 'the awakening of nature at early dawn'; 2. *Blumine – A Chapter of Flowers;* 3. (the present second movement) *Full Sail.* Part II consisted of the last two movements: 4. (the present third movement) *Left in the Lurch – Funeral March in the Manner of Callot –* 'The Huntsman's Funeral'; 5. (finale) *Dall' Inferno al Paradiso,* the beginning being 'the sudden outburst of a wounded heart'.

The title and programme were contradictions: Mahler came to detest all programmes, and eventually withdrew those of his first three symphonies. Yet he always insisted that his music was *about* something. He once wrote about his first two symphonies: 'My whole life is contained in them: I have set down in them my experience and suffering . . . to anyone who knows how to listen, my whole life will become clear, for my creative works and my existence are so closely interwoven that, if my life flowed as peacefully as a stream through a meadow, I believe I would no longer be able to compose anything.'

*

In the hushed slow introduction to the first movement, a seven-octave A on strings evokes the infinitude of nature, and a falling fourth grows into a basic theme. But reality – military fanfares and cuckoo calls – intrudes immediately, presenting Mahler's vision of childhood – memories of early awakenings at dawn. Romantic horn phrases voice nostalgia, regret for lost innocence. Soon the world awakes, and (first movement proper) the 'wayfaring lad' is off across the countryside, to the D major *Fahrenden Gesellen* 'walking tune': * lively pastoral exposition, animated climax – and return of the introduction. Tranquillity again; the heat of noonday. Sadness creeps in (cellos, D minor), and awe at the mysterious stillness, intensified by birdsong in the foreground. (Mahler's father once left him alone in the woods, telling him not to move till he returned; the return was delayed for hours, but Mahler was still sitting there, lost in a day-dream.) Horn calls awaken the dreamer (development): the 'walking tune' jogs the sad cello theme along in genial major form. But suddenly the sad theme tautens into new, anxious material (F minor); images of cruelty and pain arise, threateningly; tense march rhythms sweep the music to a terrifying climax. At the last moment, however, the trumpet fanfares burst in, to wrench the climax into a resplendent D major: joy in the glory of nature obliterates dread and anguish. The 'walking tune' returns for an exuberant recapitulation.

The A major Ländler, with its stampings and yodellings (partly out of 'Hans und Grete'), and its clattering trumpets and whooping horns, conjures up the primitive pleasures of country life, witnessed so often in childhood; the F major trio voices again the longing to return.

In the D minor third movement, this pastoral world is invaded by Death the annihilator, portrayed with grotesque irony as a spectre in some eerie fairy tale. Still presenting the Whole Truth, Mahler makes a sinister funeral march out of a children's nursery tune, the German variant of 'Frère Jacques' – 'Brother Martin, are you sleeping?' Over muffled drum-beats, the tune, whined sepulchrally by a muted solo double bass, is taken up in ghostly canon. A toy-like fanfare on the oboe adds bitter poignancy; cheap band music a sense of life's tawdriness. The G major trio offers the romantic 'consoling' view of death, to the closing strains of the *Fahrenden Gesellen* cycle; but the spectre marches back, emphasizing more strongly the idea of annihilation before fading into darkness.

The finale breaks in immediately with (as Mahler said) 'the cry of a wounded heart': a dissonant scream on wind and brass, followed by the first movement's anxiety music, intensified into horror by the preceding vision of death, and permeated with a vehement brass figure (four descending chromatic notes). The main movement begins with a battling version of the first movement's F minor march; this, after much striving, collapses with despairing statements of the vehement brass figure; and a yearning melody in D flat emerges, craving consolation. The march returns implacably; a momentary premonition of triumph interrupts it – a quiet transformation of the march motive into a brave C major fanfare, and of the vehement brass figure into a confident processional tune – only to be swept away. But eventually the fanfare

* All the interpretations of the symphonies in this book are *symbolic* – the music expresses not actual events but the moods connected with them.

breaks through again in C, on full brass, and with a breath-taking key-switch hurls the movement victoriously into the symphony's true key – D major. A triumphal march begins with the confident processional tune, joined by a militant version of the symphony's opening 'nature' motive; when it comes to a peaceful close, the first movement's introduction returns nostalgic-ally, followed by the finale's yearning theme – which allows the anxiety music to slip back in F minor. This time it is obliterated by the same D major climax as in the first movement, and the symphony marches to a swaggeringly triumphant conclusion, with a clangorous contrapuntal combination of themes on full brass. The music, tremendously exultant, is deliberately in 'popular' style. In this first conflict, the young Mahler wrested from nostalgia and anguish a healthy confidence in life – his own life, real life, not an artistic abstraction.

LIEDER UND GESÄNGE (VOLS. 2 AND 3), *nine songs with piano* (*c. 1887–90*).

These mark an important stage in Mahler's development, being settings of poems from the treasury of German folk poetry *Des Knaben Wunderhorn (The Youth's Magic Horn)*, which he knew from childhood, and which was to inspire him for fourteen years. This recourse to the wellspring of primitive feeling brought new 'popular' elements into Mahler's style: the pure military funeral march complete with military fanfares, in 'Zu Strassburg auf der Schanz' ' (a valediction of a deserter facing execution); a pert humour, in 'Um schlimme Kinder' and 'Starke Einbildungskraft'; and an indescribably quaint drollery, in 'Ablösung im Sommer' (which tells with gawky mock pathos of the cuckoo's death, and with naïve mock merriment of the luckily still-living nightingale). This new humorous vein will fertilize the symphonies.

Lieder und Gesänge, Volume 2

UM SCHLIMME KINDER ARTIG ZU MACHEN	TO TEACH NAUGHTY CHILDREN TO BE GOOD
Es kam ein Herr zum Schlösseli auf einem schönen Rösseli, Ku-kukuk, ku-kukuk, ku-kukuk!	*There came a gentleman to a castle, riding on a fine mare. Cu-cuckoo, cu-cuckoo, cu-cuckoo.*
Da lugt die Frau zum Fenster aus und sagt: "der Mann ist nicht zu Haus. und niemand heim als meine Kind', und's Mädchen ist auf der Wäschewind! "	*The lady, looking out of the window, says: 'My husband's out, nobody's home but the children, and the maid is away washing.'*

Der Herr auf seinem Rösseli
sagt zu der Frau im Schlösseli:
Ku-kukuk, ku-kukuk, ku-kukuk!

"Sind's gute Kind', sind's böse Kind'?
Ach, liebe Frau, ach sagt geschwind",
Ku-kukuk, ku-kukuk, ku-kukuk!

"In meiner Tasch' für folgsam Kind',
da hab' ich manche Angebind' ",
Ku-kukuk, ku-kukuk, ku-kukuk!

Die Frau die sagt: "sehr böse Kind'!
Sie folgen Muttern nicht geschwind,
sind böse!"

Da sagt der Herr: "so reit' ich heim,
dergleichen Kinder brauch' ich kein'!"
Ku-kukuk, ku-kukuk, ku-kukuk!

Und reit' auf seinem Rösseli
weit entweg vom Schlösseli!
Ku-kukuk, ku-kukuk, ku-kukuk!

(*from* Des Knaben Wunderhorn)

The gentleman on his mare
says to the lady of the castle:
Cu-cuckoo, cu-cuckoo, cu-cuckoo.

'Are the children good or naughty?
Come, dear lady, tell me quickly',
Cu-cuckoo, cu-cuckoo, cu-cuckoo.

'In my pocket I have goodies
for obedient children.'
Cu-cuckoo, cu-cuckoo, cu-cuckoo.

The lady says: 'Very bad children –
they won't obey their mother –
they're wicked!'

The gentleman says: 'Well, I'll ride home,
I don't want anything to do with children
like that!'
Cu-cuckoo, cu-cuckoo, cu-cuckoo.

And rode away on his mare
far away from the castle.
Cu-cuckoo, cu-cuckoo, cu-cuckoo.

ICH GING MIT LUST DURCH EINEN GRÜNEN WALD

FULL OF JOY I WALKED THROUGH A GREEN WOOD

Ich ging mit Lust durch einen grünen Wald,
ich hört' die Vöglein singen.
Sie sangen so jung, sie sangen so alt,
die kleinen Waldvögelein im grünen Wald!
Wie gern' hört' ich sie singen, ja singen!

Nun sing', nun sing', Frau Nachtigall!
Sing' du's bei meinem Feinsliebchen:
'Komm schier, komm schier, wenn's finster
    ist,
wenn niemand auf der Gasse ist,
dann komm' zu mir, dann komm' zu mir!
Herein will ich dich lassen, ja lassen!'

Der Tag verging, die Nacht brach an,
er kam zu Feinsliebchen gegangen,
Er klopft so leis' wohl an den Ring,
ei, schläfst du oder wachst, mein Kind?
Ich hab' so lang' gestanden!

Full of joy I walked through a green wood
and listened to the birds' song.
They sang, young ones, old ones,
little woodbirds in the green wood.
How nice to hear them singing, yes singing!

Please sing, please sing, dear nightingale,
Sing this at my beloved's place:
'Come straightway when darkness falls,
when not a soul is in the street,
then come to me, then come to me!
And I will let you in.'

The day passed by, the night began,
he came to see his sweetheart.
He knocked so gently at the door –
Hey, are you asleep or awake, my child?
I've been waiting so long.

Es schaut der Mond durch's Fensterlein	*The moon looked through the little window*
zum holden, süssen Lieben,	*on the charming, sweet caresses.*
die Nachtigall sang die ganze Nacht.	*The nightingale sang throughout the night.*
Du schlafselig' Mägdelein, nimm dich	*You blissfully sleeping maiden, beware!*
in Acht!	*Where now is your lover?*
Wo ist dein Herzliebster geblieben?	

(*from* Des Knaben Wunderhorn)

AUS! AUS!   FINISHED! FINISHED!

'Heute marschieren wir!
Juchhe, juchhe, im grünen Mai!
Morgen marschieren wir
zu dem hohen Tor hinaus! Aus!'

Today we'll march.
Hurrah, hurrah, in May so green!
Tomorrow we'll march through the high
gate.

' "Reis'st du denn schon fort?
Je, je! Mein Liebster!
Kommst niemals wieder heim?
Je! Je! Mein Liebster?" '

'Do you already depart, my love?
And never will return, my love?'

'Heute marschieren wir,
juchhe, juchhe im grünen Mai!
Ei, du schwarzbraun's Mägdelein,
uns're Lieb' ist noch nicht aus, aus!

Today we'll march,
hurrah, hurrah, in May so green!
Hey, my dark-haired girl,
our love is far from finished, finished!

Trink' du ein Gläschen Wein
zur Gesundheit dein und mein!
Siehst du diesen Strauss am Hut?
Jetzo heisst's marschieren gut!
Nimm das Tüchlein aus der Tasch',
deine Tränlein mit abwasch'!

Drink a glass of wine
to your health and mine!
Do you see the flowers on my hat?
That means: we march.
Take your hankie out of your pocket
to wipe your tears away.

Heute marschieren wir,
juchhe, juchhe, im grünen Mai!

Today we'll march,
hurrah, hurrah, in May so green!

' "Ich will in's Kloster geh'n,
weil mein Schatz davon geht!
Wo geht's denn hin, mein Schatz?
Gehst du fort, heut schon fort?
Und kommst nimmer wieder?
Ach! Wie wird's traurig sein
hier in dem Städtchen!
Wie bald vergisst du mein!
Ich! armes Mädchen!" '

'I'll enter a convent
since my love is going away.
Where then are you going, my love?
Are you going away, already today?
And never to return?
Ah, how sad it will be,
here in the town.
How soon you'll forget me!
Me, poor girl!'

'Morgen marschieren wir,

Tomorrow we'll march,

juchhe, juchhe, im grünen Mai!	*hurrah, hurrah, in May so green!*
Tröst' dich, mein lieber Schatz,	*Console yourself, my darling love,*
im Mai blüh'n gar viel Blümelein!	*many flowers bloom in May –*
Die Lieb' ist noch nicht aus! Aus! Aus!'	*our love is not yet finished! Finished!*

(*from* Des Knaben Wunderhorn)

STARKE EINBILDUNGSKRAFT   STRONG IMAGINATION

MÄDCHEN:
Hast gesagt, du willst mich nehmen,
sobald der Sommer kommt!
Der Sommer ist gekommen, ja kommen,
du hast mich nicht genommen, ja nommen!
Geh', Büble, geh'! Geh', nehm' mich!
Gelt, ja? Du nimmst mich noch?

GIRL:
You've said that you'll take me
as soon as summer comes.
Well summer's come all right
and you haven't taken me –
Go on boy – go on, take me!
Won't you? Aren't you going to take me?

BÜBLE:
Wie soll ich dich denn nehmen,
dieweil ich dich schon hab'?
Und wenn ich halt an dich gedenk',
so mein' ich alleweile:
ich wär' schon bei dir!

BOY:
How should I take you.
When I already have you all the time?
And when I think of you
then all the time it seems to me
as if I was already with you!

(*from* Des Knaben Wunderhorn)

Lieder und Gesänge, Volume 3

ZU STRASSBURG AUF DER SCHANZ'   ON THE RAMPARTS OF STRASSBURG

Zu Strassburg auf der Schanz',
da ging mein Trauern an!
Das Alphorn hört' ich drüben wohl
anstimmen,
in's Vaterland musst' ich hinüber
schwimmen;
das ging ja nicht an!

On the ramparts of Strassburg
my calamity began.
I heard the sound of the alp-horn from over
the border,
I had to swim over to my homeland –
that was not allowed!

Ein' Stund' in der Nacht
sie haben mich gebracht;
sie führten mich gleich vor des Hauptmann's
Haus! Ach Gott!
Sie fischten mich im Strome aus!
Mit mir ist es aus!

In the middle of the night
I was caught,
and led at once to the captain's quarters.
They fished me out of the river! God!
I don't stand a chance!

Früh morgens um zehn Uhr
stellt man mich vor's Regiment!
Ich soll da bitten um Pardon!
Und ich bekomm' doch meinen Lohn!
Das weiss ich schon!

Ihr Brüder all' zumal,
heut' seht ihr mich zum letzten mal!
Der Hirtenbub' ist nur schuld daran!
Das Alphorn hat mir's angetan!
Das klag' ich an!

(*from* Des Knaben Wunderhorn)

Early morning, at ten o'clock
I'll be court-martialled in front of the regiment.
I should ask for pardon,
but I'll get my reward!
That much I know!

You brothers, everywhere,
Today you'll see me for the last time.
It's all the shepherd boy's fault,
and the alp-horn's doing!
That is my plaint!

ABLÖSUNG IM SOMMER

THE CHANGING OF THE SUMMER GUARD

Kukuk hat sich zu Tode gefallen,
an einer grünen Weiden!
Kukuk ist tot! hat sich zu Tod' gefallen!
Wer soll uns denn den Sommer lang
die Zeit und Weil' vertreiben?

Ei! Das soll tun Frau Nachtigall!
Die sitzt auf grünem Zweige!
Die kleine, feine Nachtigall,
die liebe, süsse Nachtigall!
Sie singt und springt, ist all' zeit froh,
wenn andre Vögel schweigen!

Wir warten auf Frau Nachtigall;
die wohnt im grünen Hage,
und wenn der Kukuk zu Ende ist,
dann fängt sie an zu schlagen!

(*from* Des Knaben Wunderhorn)

Cuckoo has collided with a green willow-
tree,
cuckoo is dead – he lies dead!
Who should pass away the time for us all
summer long?

Ah! Mrs Nightingale will do that –
She sits on the green branch,
that small and graceful nightingale,
that lovely and sweet nightingale.
She hops and sings, she's cheerful all the time,
when other birds are silent.

We're waiting for Mrs Nightingale,
she lives in the green copse
and when the cuckoo's time is up
she'll start singing!

SCHEIDEN UND MEIDEN

FAREWELL AND FORGO

Es ritten drei Reiter zum Tore hinaus!
Ade! Ade!
Fein's Liebchen, das schaute zum Fenster
    hinaus!
Ade! Ade! Ade!

Und wenn es denn soll geschieden sein,

Three riders rode away from the gate.
Adieu! Adieu!
The sweetheart looked down from the
window.
Adieu!

If then we have to part,

so reich' mir dein goldenes Ringelein!
Ja, Scheiden und Meiden tut weh, tut weh!

pass to me your golden ring.
Yes, to say farewell and forgo causes pain!

Es scheidet das Kind schon in der Wieg'!
Wann werd' ich mein Schätzel wohl
   kriegen?!

The child in the cradle says already farewell,
When will I have my darling?

Und ist es nicht morgen, ach, wär' es doch
   heut'!
Es machte uns Beiden wohl grosse Freud'!
Ja, Scheiden und Meiden tut weh, tut weh!
Ade!

As it won't be tomorrow, I wish it were
*   today!*
It would make both of us so happy.
Yes, to say farewell and forgo causes pain!
Adieu!

(*from* Des Knaben Wunderhorn)

NICHT WIEDERSEHEN!

NEVER TO MEET AGAIN

Und nun ade, mein herzallerliebster Schatz!
Jetzt muss ich wohl scheiden von dir,
bis auf den andern Sommer,
dann komm' ich wieder zu dir! Ade!

Now farewell, my beloved treasure,
I have to part from you
till the summer after next,
then I shall return to you. Farewell!

Und als der junge Knab' heimkam,
von seiner Liebsten fing er an:
"Wo ist meine Herzallerliebste,
die ich verlassen hab'?"

When the boy came back,
he asked for his sweetheart:
'Where is the darling love
I left behind?'

"Auf dem Kirchhof liegt sie begraben,
heut' ist's der dritte Tag!
Das Trauern und das Weinen
hat sie zum Tod gebracht!"

'She was buried in the churchyard three days
*   ago.*
Grief and tears caused her death.'

Ade, ade, mein herzallerliebster Schatz!
Jetzt will ich auf den Kirchhof geh'n,
will suchen meiner Liebsten Grab,
will ihr all'weile rufen,
bis dass sie mir Antwort gab!

Farewell, my beloved treasure!
Now I will go to the churchyard
to look for my darling's grave,
to call for her incessantly until she answers
*   me.*

Ei du, mein allerherzliebster Schatz,
mach' auf dein tiefes Grab!
Du hörst kein Glöcklein läuten,
du hörst kein Vöglein pfeifen,
du siehst weder Sonne noch Mond!
Ade, mein herzallerliebster Schatz! Ade!

Oh you, my beloved darling,
open your deep grave!
You no longer hear the bells ringing,
you no longer hear the birds singing,
you no longer see sun or moon.
Farewell, my beloved!

(*from* Des Knaben Wunderhorn)

SELBSTGEFÜHL	SELF-ASSURANCE
Ich weiss nicht, wie mir ist!	*I don't know what's the matter with me!*
Ich bin nicht krank und nicht gesund,	*I'm not ill and I'm not well,*
ich bin blessirt und hab' kein' Wund',	*I'm wounded, but have no scar,*
ich weiss nicht, wie mir ist!	*I don't know what's the matter with me!*
Ich tät' gern essen und schmeckt mir nichts;	*I should like to eat, but taste nothing,*
ich hab' ein Geld und gilt mir nichts,	*I've got some money, for which I don't care,*
ich weiss nicht, wie mir ist!	*I don't know what's the matter with me!*
Ich hab' sogar kein' Schnupftabak,	*Maybe, I haven't even a pinch of snuff,*
und hab' kein' Kreuzer Geld im Sack!	*Maybe, I haven't even a farthing in my*
Ich weiss nicht wie mir ist, wie mir ist!	* pocket,*
	I don't know what's the matter with me!
Heiraten tät' ich auch schon gern',	*I'd really like to get married,*
kann aber Kinderschrei'n nicht hör'n!	*but I can't bear the sound of children crying.*
Ich weiss nicht, wie mir ist!	*I don't know what's the matter with me!*
Ich hab' erst heut den Doktor gefragt,	*Only today I asked the doctor*
der hat mir's in's Gesicht gesagt:	*and he told me bluntly:*
"Ich weiss wohl, was dir ist:	*'I know what's the matter with you:*
Ein Narr bist du gewiss! "	*You're a fool!'*
' "Nun weiss ich, wie mir ist! " '	*'Now I know what's the matter with me!'*

(*from* Des Knaben Wunderhorn)

DES KNABEN WUNDERHORN, *ten orchestral songs* (1892–9).
   In this unique set of masterpieces, the moods and styles sketched in the preceding piano songs come to perfect fruition, and are superbly characterized by a new, graphic style of instrumentation. The (smallish) orchestra varies according to expressive need: from single wind and horn to double wind, four horns, one or two trumpets and timpani; no heavy brass, but occasionally military percussion. But whatever the size of the orchestra, it is always used in chamber style, each part standing out like a line in an engraving.
   The thematic style is basic and vastly appealing. As Richard Specht said, 'in earlier centuries, such songs may have been sung in small market towns among soldiers, shepherds, and peasants.' Two are trance-like night scenes alternating military music with Ländler: 'Der Schildwache Nachtlied', in which a sentry is killed on duty while dreaming of his sweetheart; and 'Wo die schönen Trompeten blasen', in which a dead soldier's ghost (fanfares on

muted brass and soft woodwind) visits his sleeping beloved (a melting Ländler for strings). The 'Lied des Verfolgten im Turm' contrasts grim martial strains with pathetic pastoral music, picturing the unbroken spirit of a political prisoner, haunted by hallucinations of summer meadows; 'Trost im Unglück' is a lively duet between a Hussar and his erstwhile girlfriend. Two are subtilized Ländler: the wheedling 'Verlor'ne Müh'' presents a bashful village girl wooing an unresponsive swain; the lilting 'Rheinlegendchen' a charming fairy-tale. Two are utterly 'crazy': the bumbling 'Lob des hohen Verstandes', telling how the ass, judging a singing contest, rates the cuckoo above the nightingale; and the nonsensical 'Wer hat dies Liedel erdacht?', a Ländler introducing a new Mahlerian feature – the flowing *moto perpetuo*. This procedure is used to sinister effect in the two most remarkable songs. In 'Das irdische Leben', telling of a child dying of starvation while the mill grinds the corn too late, an oscillating *moto perpetuo* represents the mill – and symbolically the 'treadmill' of life; in 'Des Antonius von Padua Fischpredigt', a sardonic account of St Anthony's futile sermon to the fishes (who swam away as heedless and greedy as before), a gliding ostinato represents the swimming fish – and symbolically the restless, automatic, purposeless busyness of life.

Material from the *Wunderhorn* songs will be used in the Second and Third Symphonies – which raises an important point. Mahler was no 'song-symphonist', in the sense of an inflator of lyrical material to monumental proportions; his songs flower naturally into symphonic movements, being already symphonic in cast. His approach is rarely lyrical like Schubert, never declamatory like Wolf. He uses the poems freely as a basis for brief 'movements' built out of short motives: the texts are often lopped or modified, the words repeated or drawn out to fit the thematic development; the voice is just one more instrument (a highly expressive one) in the motivic texture.

DER SCHILDWACHE NACHTLIED	SENTRY'S NIGHT-SONG
SCHILDWACHE:	SENTRY:
Ich kann und mag nicht fröhlich sein!	*I can't and won't be cheerful here!*
Wenn alle Leute schlafen,	*When everyone is sleeping,*
so muss ich wachen! Ja wachen!	*I must be watching, be watching.*
Muss traurig sein!	*It's cheerless here!*
MÄDCHEN:	GIRL:
Lieb' Knabe, du musst nicht traurig sein!	*Dear boy, you mustn't be so sad!*
Will deiner warten im Rosengarten,	*I'll wait for you in the rose-garden,*
im grünen Klee,	*in clover green,*
im grünen Klee!	*in clover green.*

SCHILDWACHE:	SENTRY:
Zum grünen Klee da geh' ich nicht!	*In clover green – that's not my place!*
Zum Waffengarten voll Helleparten	*The field of battle where halberds flourish –*
bin ich gestellt!	*that is my post!*

MÄDCHEN:	GIRL:
Stehst du im Feld, so helf' dir Gott!	*The field of battle – may God be your guide!*
An Gottes Segen ist alles gelegen!	*In God's good keeping are all things human,*
Wer's glauben tut!	*for one with faith.*
Wer's glauben tut!	*For one with faith.*

SCHILDWACHE:	SENTRY:
Wer's glauben tut, ist weit davon!	*The one with faith is far from here.*
Er ist ein König! Er ist ein Kaiser, ein	*He is a monarch, a Kaiser, a Kaiser!*
Kaiser!	*He wages war! – Halt! Who goes there?*
Er führt den Krieg! – Halt! Wer da!! Rund'!	*Patrol!*
Bleib' mir vom Leib!	*Keep off from me!*

Wer sang es hier? Wer sang zur Stund'?	*What song was here? Who sang just now?*
Verlorne Feldwacht sang es um Mitternacht!	*Forlorn, a sentry sang it at midnight!*
Mitternacht! Mitternacht! Feldwacht!	*Midnight! Midnight! Sentry!*

VERLOR'NE MÜH'	WASTED EFFORT
SIE:	SHE:
Büble . . . wir!	*Laddie, why . . .*
Büble, wir wollen aussegehe! aussegehe!	*Laddie, why don't we go a-walking,*
Wollen wir? Wollen wir? Unsere Lämmer	*a-walking?*
besehe!	*Shall we now? Shall we now? See how our*
Gelt! Komm'!	*lambkins are faring?*
Komm'! lieb's Büberle, komm', ich bitt'!	*Yes? Come!*
	Come, dear laddie, O come, I beg!

ER:	HE:
Närrisches Dinterle, ich mag dich halt nit!	*Stupid young lassie, I have no time for you!*

SIE:	SHE:
Willst vielleicht . . .	*Would you like . . .*
Willst vielleicht a bissel nasche? bissel	*Would you like a little nibble? little nibble?*
nasche?	*Would you now? Would you now?*
Willst vielleicht? Willst vielleicht?	*Take a bit from my pocket!*
Hol' dir was aus meiner Tasch'!	*Take something! Take something!*
Hol' dir was! Hol' dir was!	*Take! Take!*
Hol'! Hol'!	*Take, dear laddie, O take, I beg!*
Hol', lieb's Büberle, hol', ich bitt'!	

ER:	HE:
Närrisches Dinterle, ich nasch' dir halt nit!	*Stupid young lassie, I won't take your*
	bait!

44

SIE:
Gelt? Ich soll ...
Gelt? Ich soll mein Herz dir schenke?
Herz dir schenke?
Gelt? ich soll? Gelt? ich soll?
Immer willst an mich gedenke?
Immer! Immer! Immer!
Nimm's! Nimm's!
Nimm's, lieb's Büberle! Nimm's, ich bitt'!

ER:
Närrisches Dinterle, ich mag es halt nit!

SHE:
Tell me, shall ...
Tell me, shall I give my heart then,
give my heart then?
Shall I now? Shall I now?
So I shall be yours for ever?
Ever! Ever! Ever!
Take! Take!
Take, dear laddie, O take, I beg!

HE:
Stupid young lassie, I do not want your
heart!

TROST IM UNGLÜCK

HUSAR:
Wohlan! Die Zeit ist kommen!
Mein Pferd, das muss gesattelt sein!
Ich hab' mir's vorgenommen!
Geritten muss es sein!
Geh' du nur hin! Ich hab' mein Teil!
Ich lieb' dich nur aus Narretei!
Ohn' dich kann ich wohl leben!
Ohn' dich kann ich wohl sein!
So setz' ich mich aufs Pferdchen,
und trink' ein Gläschen kühlen Wein!
Und schwör's bei meinem Bärtchen,
dir ewig treu zu sein.

MÄDCHEN:
Du glaubst, du bist der Schönste
wohl auf der ganzen weiten Welt,
und auch der Angenehmste!
Ist aber weit, weit gefehlt!
In meines Vaters Garten
wächst eine Blume drin!
So lang will ich noch warten,
bis die noch grösser ist!
Und geh' du nur hin! Ich hab' mein Teil!
Ich lieb' dich nur aus Narretei!
Ohn' dich kann ich wohl leben!
Ohn' dich kann ich wohl sein!

HUSAR:
Du glaubst, ich werd' dich nehmen?

CONSOLATION IN
MISFORTUNE

HUSSAR:
Ah well! The time has come then!
My horse, it must be saddled now.
At last I've made my mind up
that I must ride away.
Leave me alone! I've had my fill!
I love you but from foolishness.
I can well live without you.
Without you I'll be fine!
So now I'll mount my charger,
and drink a glass of cooling wine.
But by my beard I swear it,
I'll still be true to you.

GIRL:
You think you are the fairest
of all men in the whole wide world;
and more than that, the nicest.
But there you're wrong – sadly wrong!
Within my father's garden
there grows a little flower.
And I am only waiting
until it grows quite tall.
So be on your way! I've had my fill!
I love you but from foolishness.
I can well live without you.
Without you I'll be fine!

HUSSAR:
You think that I would take you?

Das hab' lang noch nicht im Sinn!
Ich muss mich deiner schämen,
wenn ich in Gesellschaft bin!

Long since I've had no thought of that!
I'm quite ashamed of you, dear,
when I'm in company!

WER HAT DIES LIED ERDACHT?

Dort oben am Berg in dem hohen Haus,
in dem Haus,
da gucket ein fein's, lieb's Mädel heraus.
Es ist nicht dort daheime!
Es ist nicht dort daheime!
Es ist des Wirts sein Töchterlein.
Es wohnet auf grüner Haide.
Mein Herzle ist wund.
Komm', Schätzle, mach's g'sund!
Dein' schwarzbraune Äuglein,
die hab'n mich verwund't!
Dein rosiger Mund
macht Herzen gesund.
Macht Jugend verständig,
macht Tote lebendig,
macht Kranke gesund,
macht Kranke gesund,
ja, gesund.

Wer hat denn das schön schöne Liedlein
  erdacht?
Es haben's drei Gäns übers Wasser
  gebracht!
Zwei graue und eine weisse,
Zwei graue und eine weisse!
Und wer das Liedlein nicht singen kann,
dem wollen sie es pfeifen! Ja!

WHO MADE UP THIS LITTLE SONG?

Up there on the hill in the lofty house,
in the house,
a sweet darling girl stands there peeping out.
She's not really at home there,
she's not really at home there,
she is the daughter of 'mine host';
she lives up on the green heath.
My heart is so sick!
Come, dear, make it well!
Your dark brown eyes' glances
have given me a wound!
Your sweet rosy mouth
cures hearts that are sick,
makes young people clever,
gives life to the dying,
makes ill people well,
makes ill people well,
ay, well.

Who was it who made up this fine little
  song?
Three geese brought it over the water one
  day.
Two grey ones and a white one!
Two grey ones and a white one!
And anyone who can't sing the song,
they'll gladly whistle it for him! Ay!

DAS IRDISCHE LEBEN

"Mutter, ach Mutter, es hungert mich!
Gib mir Brot, sonst sterbe ich."
"Warte nur! Warte nur, mein liebes Kind!
Morgen wollen wir ernten geschwind!"

Und als das Korn geerntet war,
rief das Kind noch immerdar:
"Mutter, ach Mutter, es hungert mich!
Gib mir Brot, sonst sterbe ich!"

EARTHLY LIFE

'Mother, oh mother, how hungry I am!
Give me bread, or I shall die!'
'Wait awhile, wait awhile, my darling child!
Tomorrow the reaping will soon be done.'

But when at last the corn was reaped,
still the child cried on and on:
'Mother, oh mother, how hungry I am!
Give me bread, or I shall die!'

"Warte nur! Warte nur, mein liebes Kind!
Morgen wollen wir dreschen geschwind! "

Und als das Korn gedroschen war,
rief das Kind noch immerdar:
"Mutter, ach Mutter, es hungert mich,
gib mir Brot, sonst sterbe ich! "
"Warte nur! Warte nur, mein liebes Kind!
Morgen wollen wir backen geschwind."

Und als das Brot gebacken war,
lag das Kind auf der Totenbahr!

'Wait awhile, wait awhile, my darling child!
Tomorrow the threshing will soon be done.'

But when at last the corn was threshed,
still the child cried on and on:
'Mother, oh mother, how hungry I am!
Give me bread, or I shall die!'
'Wait awhile, wait awhile, my darling child!
Tomorrow the baking will soon be done.'

But when at last the bread was baked,
the child lay dead upon the bier.

DES ANTONIUS VON PADUA FISCHPREDIGT

Antonius zur Predigt
die Kirche find't ledig!
Er geht zu den Flüssen
und predigt den Fischen!
Sie schlag'n mit den Schwänzen!
Im Sonnenschein glänzen!

Die Karpfen mit Rogen
sind all' hierher zogen,
hab'n d' Mäuler aufrissen,
sich Zuhörn's beflissen!
Kein Predigt niemalen
den Fischen so g'fallen!

Spitzgoschete Hechte,
die immerzu fechten,
sind eilends herschwommen,
zu hören den Frommen!
Auch jene Phantasten,
die immerzu fasten:
die Stockfisch' ich meine,
zur Predigt erscheinen.
Kein Predigt niemalen
den Stockfisch so g'fallen!

Gut Aale und Hausen,
die Vornehme schmausen,
die selbst sich bequemen,
die Predigt vernehmen!
Auch Krebse, Schildkroten,
sonst langsame Boten,

ANTONY OF PADUA'S SERMON TO THE FISHES

For Anthony's sermon
the church is quite empty;
so he goes to the river
to preach to the fishes.
Their tails are all flickering,
in sunshine all glittering!

The carp, fat with roe,
in shoals are arriving,
with mouths gaping open,
to pay strict attention!
There ne'er was a sermon
the fish found so splendid!

The pike so sharp-snouted,
habitual fighters,
come hurriedly swimming,
to hear the good preacher.
Even those strange fanatics,
habitual fasters,
— it's the cod I refer to —
appear at the sermon.
There ne'er was a sermon
the cod found so splendid!

Fine eels and fine sturgeon,
devoured by the wealthy
decide to submit to
a taste of the sermon.
Even crabs, even turtles,
those wonted slow-movers,

steigen eilig vom Grund,
zu hören diesen Mund!
Kein Predigt niemalen
den Krebsen so g'fallen!
Fisch' grosse, Fisch' kleine,
vornehm und gemeine,
erheben die Köpfe,
wie verständ'ge Geschöpfe!
Auf Gottes Begehren,
die Predigt anhören!

Die Predigt geendet,
ein jener sich wendet.
Die Hechte bleiben Diebe,
die Aale viel lieben;
die Predigt hat g'fallen,
sie bleiben wie Allen!
Die Krebs geh'n zurücke;
die Stockfisch' bleib'n dicke,
die Karpfen viel fressen,
die Predigt vergessen!
Die Predigt hat g'fallen,
sie bleiben wie Allen!

shoot up from the bed,
to hear the address.
There ne'er was a sermon
the crabs found so splendid!
The large fish, the small fish,
the high-born, the low-born,
they all lift their heads up,
like rational creatures,
and on God's orders,
they listen to the sermon!

The sermon once over,
away they go swimming.
The pike to their thieving,
the eels to their loving;
the sermon was splendid,
but they're still like the others!
The crabs still move backwards,
the cod are still bloated,
the carp are still gorging,
the sermon's forgotten!
The sermon was splendid,
but they're still like the others!

RHEINLEGENDCHEN

Bald gras' ich am Neckar,
bald gras' ich am Rhein;
bald hab' ich ein Schätzel,
bald bin ich allein!
Was hilft mir das Grasen,
wenn d'Sichel nicht schneid't!
Was hilft mir ein Schätzel,
wenn's bei mir nicht bleibt!

So soll ich denn grasen
am Neckar, am Rhein,
so werf' ich mein goldenes
Ringlein hinein.
Es fliesset im Neckar
und fliesset im Rhein,
soll schwimmen hinunter
ins Meer tief hinein.

Und schwimmt es, das Ringlein,
so frisst es ein Fisch!
Das Fischlein soll kommen

LITTLE RHINE LEGEND

I mow by the Neckar,
I mow by the Rhine;
at times I've a sweetheart,
at times I'm alone.
What good is it mowing,
if the sickle won't cut?
What good is a sweetheart,
if she won't stay with me?

So if I'm to mow
by the Neckar, the Rhine,
I'll throw in their waters
my little gold ring.
It'll flow down the Neckar
and flow down the Rhine,
and float right away
to the depths of the sea.

And floating, the ring will
be gulped by a fish!
The fish will arrive

auf's Königs sein Tisch!	*as a dish for the King.*
Der König tät fragen:	*The King will enquire*
wem's Ringlein sollt' sein?	*whose ring it may be;*
Da tät mein Schatz sagen:	*my sweetheart will say*
Das Ringlein g'hört mein.	*that the ring belongs to me.*

Mein Schätzlein tät springen
Berg auf und Berg ein,
tät mir wied'rum bringen
das Goldringlein mein!
"Kannst grasen am Neckar,
kannst grasen am Rhein!
Wirf du mir nur immer
dein Ringlein hinein!"

My sweetheart will bound
over hill, over dale,
and will bring back to me
my own little gold ring.
'You can mow by the Neckar,
and mow by the Rhine,
if you'll only keep throwing
your ring in for me!'

LIED DES VERFOLGTEN IM TURM

SONG OF THE PRISONER IN THE TOWER

DER GEFANGENE:
Die Gedanken sind frei,
wer kann sie erraten,
sie rauschen vorbei
wie nächtliche Schatten,
kein Mensch kann sie wissen,
kein Jäger sie schiessen;
es bleibet dabei,
es bleibet dabei,
die Gedanken sind frei!

THE PRISONER:
Our thoughts are free,
for who can divine them?
They go rushing past
like shadows at night-time,
and no-one can know them,
no hunter can shoot them;
and so let it be,
and so let it be,
our thoughts are free!

DAS MÄDCHEN:
Im Sommer ist gut lustig sein
auf hohen, wilden Bergen.
Dort findet man grün' Plätzelein,
mein Herz verliebtes Schätzelein;
von dir mag ich nicht scheiden.

THE GIRL:
O summer is a happy time
up there in the high wild mountains.
There's many a little green nook up there,
my own most dearly beloved;
from you I won't be parted.

DER GEFANGENE:
Und sperrt man mich ein
in finstere Kerker,
dies alles sind nur,
dies alles sind nur
vergebliche Werke,
denn meine Gedanken
zerreissen die Schranken
und Mauern entzwei;
die Gedanken sind frei,
die Gedanken sind frei!

THE PRISONER:
And though I am locked
in a dismal dungeon –
whatever they do,
whatever they do,
it's all to no purpose,
because my thoughts
can shatter the bars
and walls in two;
our thoughts are free,
our thoughts are free!

DAS MÄDCHEN:	THE GIRL:

DAS MÄDCHEN:
Im Sommer ist gut lustig sein
auf hohen wilden Bergen.
Man ist da ewig ganz allein
auf hohen, wilden Bergen,
man hört da gar kein Kindergeschrei,
kein Kindergeschrei!
Die Luft mag einem da werden, ja,
die Luft mag einem werden.

THE GIRL:
O summer is a happy time
up there in the high wild mountains;
for there you're always on your own
up there in the high wild mountains,
and there you hear no children cry,
no children cry!
The air up there is refreshing, yes,
the air up there is refreshing.

DER GEFANGENE:
So sei's wie es sei,
und wenn es sich schicket,
nur alles, alles, sei in der Stille,
nur all's in der Still, all's in der Still!
Mein Wunsch und Begehren,
niemand kann's wehren!
Es bleibt dabei:
die Gedanken sind frei,
die Gedanken sind frei!

THE PRISONER:
Then so let it be,
and whatever may happen,
O let it, let it happen in secret,
in secret all, in secret all!
My wish and my longing
no-one can hinder!
And so let it be,
our thoughts are free,
our thoughts are free!

DAS MÄDCHEN:
Mein Schatz, du singst so fröhlich hier,
wie's Vögelein im Grase.
Ich steh' so traurig bei Kerkertür,
wär' ich doch tot, wär' ich bei dir;
ach muss, ach muss ich immer denn klagen?

THE GIRL:
My love, you sing as gaily here
as a bird sings in the meadows.
I stand forlorn at the prison gate,
would I were dead, or else with you,
O must I, must I mourn for ever?

DER GEFANGENE:
Und weil du so klagst,
der Lieb' ich entsage!
Und ist es gewagt,
und ist es gewagt,
so kann mich nichts plagen!
So kann ich im Herzen
stets lachen und scherzen.
Es bleibet dabei,
es bleibet dabei,
die Gedanken sind frei!

THE PRISONER:
Since you can but mourn,
my love is all over!
And now that it's done,
And now that it's done,
there's nothing can plague me!
From now, in my heart,
I'm laughing and joking.
And so let it be,
And so let it be,
our thoughts are free!

WO DIE SCHÖNEN
TROMPETEN BLASEN

WHERE THE SPLENDID
TRUMPETS ARE SOUNDING

"Wer ist denn draussen und wer klopfet an,
der mich so leise, so leise wecken kann?"

'Who's that outside there that knocks at my
door,
and who so gently, so gently wakens me?'

"Das ist der Herzallerliebste dein,
steh' auf und lass mich zu dir ein!
Was soll ich hier nun länger steh'n?
Ich seh' die Morgenröt' aufgeh'n,
die Morgenröt', zwei helle Stern'.
Bei meinem Schatz da wär' ich gern,
bei meinem Herzallerlieble! "

'It is your own true dearest love,
arise, and let me in to you!
Why leave me longer waiting here?
I see the pale red dawn appear,
the pale red dawn, and two bright stars.
Were I but only with my love,
with my own dearest beloved!'

Das Mädchen stand auf und liess ihn ein;
sie heisst ihn auch willkommen sein.
"Willkommen, lieber Knabe mein,
so lang hast du gestanden! "
Sie reicht ihm auch die schneeweisse Hand.

The girl got up and let him in,
and gladly does she welcome him.
'O welcome, dearest lad of mine,
so long you've been a-waiting!'
She gives to him her snow-white hand.

Von Ferne sang die Nachtigall;
das Mädchen fing zu weinen an.

From far off sang the nightingale;
the girl began to weep.

"Ach weine nicht, du Liebste mein,
ach weine nicht, du Liebste mein,
aufs Jahr sollst du mein Eigen sein.
Mein Eigen sollst du werden gewiss,
wie's keine sonst auf Erden ist!
O Lieb' auf grüner Erden.
Ich zieh' in Krieg auf grüne Haid',
die grüne Haide, die ist so weit.
Allwo dort die schönen Trompeten blasen,
da ist mein Haus, mein Haus von grünem
    Rasen."

'Ah do not weep, my dearest love,
ah do not weep, my dearest love,
within a year you shall be mine.
You shall be mine, my own for sure,
as no-one else upon the earth!
O love on the green earth.
I'm going to war on the green heath,
the green heath, so far away.
And there where the splendid trumpets are
    sounding,
there is my home, my home of green turf.'

LOB DES HOHEN VERSTANDES

IN PRAISE OF LOFTY INTELLECT

Einstmal in einem tiefen Tal
Kuckuck und Nachtigall
täten ein Wett' anschlagen.
Zu singen um das Meisterstück,
gewinn' es Kunst, gewinn' es Glück!
Dank soll er davon tragen!

Once in a deep and shady vale
Cuckoo and nightingale
met and made a wager,
that each would sing his masterpiece,
and one, by either skill or luck,
should prove himself the master.

Der Kuckuck sprach: "So dir's gefällt,
hab ich den Richter wählt,"
und tät gleich den Esel ernennen!
"Denn weil er hat zwei Ohren gross,
Ohren gross, Ohren gross,
so kann er hören desto bos,
und, was recht ist, kennen! "

The cuckoo said: 'If you agree,
I've found the perfect judge,'
and said that he'd chosen the donkey!
'Because he has two great big ears,
great big ears, great big ears,
he'll hear much clearer what is bad,
and he'll know what's perfect!'

Sie flogen vor den Richter bald.

They quickly flew to find the judge.

Wie dem die Sache ward erzählt,	*When they did tell him how things stood,*
schuf er, sie sollten singen!	*he bade them start their singing.*
Die Nachtigall sang lieblich aus!	*The nightingale sang gloriously!*
Der Esel sprach: "Du machst mir's kraus!	*The donkey said 'Too hard for me!*
Du machst mir's kraus! Ija! Ija!	*Too hard for me! Hee-haw! Hee-haw!*
Ich kann's in Kopf nicht bringen!"	*I just can't understand it!'*
Der Kuckuck drauf fing an geschwind	*At that the cuckoo started swift*
sein Sang durch Terz und Quart und Quint.	*his song of thirds and fourths and fifths.*
Dem Esel's g'fiels, er sprach nur: "Wart!	*The donkey liked it, and said: 'Wait! Wait!*
Wart! Wart!	*My verdict I'll deliver, deliver.*
Dein Urteil will ich sprechen, ja sprechen.	
Wohl sungen hast du, Nachtigall!	*You sang quite well there, Nightingale!*
Aber Kuckuck singst gut Choral! gut Choral.	*But Cuckoo, what a splendid tune, splendid*
und hältst den Takt fein innen, fein innen!	*tune,*
Das sprech' ich nach mein' hoh'n Verstand,	*And such a nice firm tempo, firm tempo!*
hoh'n Verstand,	*So says my lofty intellect, intellect,*
und kost' es gleich ein ganzes Land,	*intellect,*
so lass ich's dich gewinnen, gewinnen."	*and even if it costs the earth*
Kuckuck, Kuckuck, Ija!	*I make you out the winner, the winner.'*
	Cuckoo! Cuckoo! Hee-haw!

———

SYMPHONY NO. 2 ('RESURRECTION'), *for soprano, contralto, chorus, orchestra and organ; composed 1888–94; first performed in Berlin, 1895, Mahler conducting.*

For this revolutionary work, he used a large orchestra (ten horns, eight trumpets, much percussion); a vast time-scale (eighty-five minutes); five movements (one with solo voice, the finale with soloists, chorus, and off-stage band); and a progressive tonality from C minor to E flat. Again the original programme was withdrawn; but the title stands, deriving from the finale's text – Klopstock's 'Resurrection Ode' – and the programme is useful as a guide.

✳

Several of Mahler's symphonies embody a struggle with some spiritual problem which is eventually resolved in the finale. In the Second, the problem is that of finding some assurance in the face of human mortality; and the resolution is a reaffirmation of the Christian belief in resurrection and immortality. This 'meaning' is conveyed clearly by the symphony itself; but Mahler ratified it in a verbal 'programme' which he drew up for the work in 1896, four months after its first performance, at the request of a young composer and journalist, Max Marschalk, who was one of his earliest admirers.

At first, he was unwilling to satisfy the young man's curiosity, insisting that the symphony spoke for itself. He wrote to Marschalk:

I should regard my work as having completely failed, if I found it necessary to give people like yourself even an indication as to its mood-sequence. In my conception of the work, I was in no way concerned with the detailed setting forth of an *event*, but much rather of a *feeling*. The conceptual basis of the work is spoken out clearly in the words of the final chorus, and the sudden emergence of the contralto solo [the fourth movement] throws an illuminating light on the earlier movements.

After several protests, however, Mahler consented to put into words the idea behind the symphony. He wrote as follows:

I have named the first movement 'Todtenfeier' [Funeral Rites, or Obsequies], and if you want to know, it is the hero of my D major symphony [No. 1] whom I bear to the grave there, and whose life I catch up, from a higher standpoint, in a pure mirror. At the same time there is the great question: 'Why did you live? Why did you suffer? Is it all nothing but a huge, frightful joke?' We *must* answer these questions in some way, if we want to go on living – indeed, if we are to go on dying! He into whose life this call has once sounded must give an answer; and this answer I give in the final movement.

The second and third movements are conceived as an interlude. The second is a memory – a shaft of sunlight from out of the life of this hero. It has surely happened to you, that you have followed a loved one to the grave, and then perhaps, on the way back, there suddenly arose the image of a long-dead hour of happiness, which now enters your soul like a sunbeam that nothing can obscure – you could almost forget what has just happened. That is the second movement.

But when you awake from this wistful dream, and have to return into the confusion of life, it can easily happen that this ever-moving, never-resting, never-comprehensible bustle of existence becomes horrible to you, like the swaying of dancing figures in a brightly-lit ballroom, into which you look from the dark night outside – and from such a great *distance* that you can no longer hear the music. Life strikes you as meaningless, a frightful ghost, from which you perhaps start away with a cry of disgust. This is the third movement; what follows is surely clear to you.

Five years later, for a Dresden performance, Mahler drew up another programme, this time for public consumption. His explanation of the first three movements was along exactly the same lines as before, but it was now followed by a commentary on the rest of the symphony:

Fourth Movement: the morning voice of ingenuous faith strikes on our ears.

Fifth Movement: we are confronted once more with terrifying questions. A voice is heard crying aloud: 'The end of all living things is come – the Last Judgement is at hand'. . . . The earth quakes, the graves burst open, the dead arise and stream on in endless procession. The great and the little ones of the earth – kings and beggars, righteous and godless – all press on; the cry for mercy and forgiveness strikes fearfully on our ears. The wailing rises higher – our senses desert us, consciousness fails at the approach of the eternal spirit. The last trumpet is heard – the trumpets of the Apocalypse ring out; in the eerie silence which follows, we can just catch the distant, barely audible song of a nightingale, a last tremulous echo of earthly life.

A chorus of saints and heavenly beings softly breaks forth: 'Thou shalt arise, surely thou shalt arise.' Then appears the glory of God: a wondrous soft light penetrates us to the heart – all is holy calm.

And behold, it is no judgement; there are no sinners, no just. None is great, none small. There is no punishment and no reward. An overwhelming love illuminates our being. We know and *are*.

On the very day of the performance, however, Mahler had a revulsion back to his earlier distrust of programmes. He wrote to his wife:

I only drew up the programme as a crutch for a cripple (you know who I mean). It can give only a superficial indication, all that any programme can do for a musical work. . . . In fact, as religious doctrines do, it leads directly to a flattening and coarsening, and in the long run to such distortion that the work . . . is utterly unrecognizable.

In view of Mahler's ambivalent attitude towards his programme, what value can it have for us today? Some modern musicians would advise us to ignore it altogether – quoting Mahler's own disparagement of it as the best reason – and to experience the symphony purely as 'absolute music', as so much fascinating melody, harmony, rhythm, orchestration and form. But this seems impossible, since the work itself contains its own programme: the last two movements have explicit verbal texts, while the wordless first movement mounts an assault on our emotions which we can hardly ignore. In any case, Mahler himself would not have agreed with this point of view. In the same letter to Marschalk he wrote:

We find ourselves faced with the important question how, and indeed *why* music should be interpreted in words at all. . . . As long as my experience can be summed up in words, I write no music about it; my need to express myself musically – symphonically – begins at the point where the *dark* feelings hold sway, at the door which leads into the 'other world' – the world in which things are no longer separated by space and time.

Clearly then, Mahler expected us to experience the symphony, not at all as absolute music, but as the musical expression of feelings too mysterious and deep-seated to be described in words, even his own, without being distorted. But this would demand an ideal listener, who could so immediately respond to the feelings in the music as to have no need of reflection or clarification. Many a music-lover likes to analyse the feelings that music awakens in him; moreover, those who are puzzled by the work may need some indication as to the general *area* of feeling the music is concerned with. What we should do, perhaps, is neither reject Mahler's programme, nor take it literally, but try to penetrate to its valid psychological core, shearing away all inessentials.

To begin with, the later addition, concerning the last two movements, is strictly redundant. In the fourth movement, the *Wunderhorn* song 'Urlicht' ('Primeval Light'), both the folk poem and its hymn-like setting proclaim explicitly their 'ingenuous faith'; and the vivid tone-painting in the finale portrays unmistakably the image of the Day of Judgement, while the final chorale-like setting of Klopstock's 'Resurrection Ode' (with even more explicit verses added by Mahler himself) also speaks for itself. (Mahler had actually stressed all this in his letter to Marschalk, as we have seen.) And the final paragraph, about there being 'no judgement', is not only redundant, but irrelevant: Mahler was no doubt carried away by writing about the concept of an afterlife into adding a purely doctrinal view, which he happened to hold at the time, but which has no bearing on the symphony at all. Indeed, it may well have been his later realization of this which caused his revulsion from the whole programme – a conjecture which finds support in an amusing anecdote in his wife's book:

> There was a beautiful old lady of hysterical tendencies, who . . . when Mahler was in Russia . . . summoned him and told him that she felt her death to be near, and would he enlighten her about the other world, as he had said so much about it in his Second Symphony. He was not so well informed about it as she supposed, and he was made to feel very distinctly, when he took his leave, that she was displeased with him.

How should Mahler have known anything about the nature of the after-life, or even whether there was such a thing? In his last two movements he had simply expressed, in symbolic terms, his own *faith* – in God, resurrection and eternal life; and they need no programme, nor any doctrinal gloss.

The 'resurrection' finale links back, thematically and emotionally, with the large opening movement; and according to Mahler's programme, it 'answers the questions' of this movement. But it is rather the questions of Mahler's *programme* ('Why did you live? Why did you suffer? Is it all nothing but a huge, frightful joke?') which are answered by part of the *text* he himself added to Klopstock's Ode for his finale ('O believe, thou wert not born in vain, hast not lived in vain, suffered in vain'). Obviously, a purely orchestral movement cannot ask questions, because music by itself is incapable of doing so. If Mahler had not drawn up his programme, we should have had no idea that it was intended to ask questions at all.

It is here that we have to look beyond Mahler's loose phraseology to the psychological reality behind it. The first movement has the rhythm and character of a funeral march, but a quicker tempo; and whereas the normal funeral march is a dignified expression of grief, Mahler's movement is full of anger, revolt, and wild despair. It clearly expresses the state of mind of one who feels a sense of outrage at the apparent omnipotence of death, and can find no ultimate significance in human life in the face of it – a state of mind which implies the 'questions' in the programme.

The same approach is necessary with Mahler's curious phrase 'it is the hero of my D major symphony whom I bear to the grave there'. A symphony cannot have a hero, and its composer cannot bear him to the grave in the next symphony. But programme symphonies of this kind deal in universal statements about mortal humanity, and the 'hero' of a Mahler symphony is simply

Mahler's projection in his own mind of the person whom these statements concern: Everyman, or at least every man in the same predicament as Mahler. Mahler's phrase was only a symbolic way of saying that in the First Symphony the universal implications of the funeral march (the third movement in this case) are eventually swept aside and ignored in the finale through an affirmation of youthful vitality and confidence; but in the Second Symphony these implications are 'caught up from a higher standpoint' – i.e. confronted on the metaphysical plane and resolved by an act of religious faith.

The programme's description of the second and third movements confronts us with visual images, but again we must penetrate to their underlying psychological meaning. The images of the memory at the graveside and the far-off inaudible ballroom music are poetic analogies indicating that the first movement's vision of death's omnipotence is followed by a two-movement interlude concerned with life – its happiness and its bitterness. For these Mahler, as so often, used the Austrian country dance, the Ländler, to symbolize the 'dance of life'. But the first movement's overpowering character has the effect of shrinking the vision of life's happiness here to a small space, and to a subdued and fragile thing. The second movement is a short slow Ländler, basically wistful in mood and eventually overshadowed by an intrusion of the first movement's angry atmosphere (in the second statement of its trio section); this reduces the final statement of the wistful Ländler section to a disembodied ghost of itself (though it later regains its substance).

In the third movement, the scherzo, Mahler uses the quicker type of Ländler for his vision of life's bitterness – total bitterness, according to his programme, though most admirers of the symphony sense other feelings there as well – genial vitality, humour and longing. The relentless twisting and twining of the main material certainly has something sinister about it, but something comical as well; in fact Mahler lifted it bodily from his amusing *Wunderhorn* song 'St Anthony of Padua's Sermon to the Fishes'. And in the two trio sections there is some exuberant popular dance music and a hauntingly nostalgic passage for four trumpets in close harmony.

Yet the general effect of the movement, in the context of the whole symphony, is without doubt that of a complacently persistent busy-ness, on a plane of easy pleasure, which does at times take on a macabre shadowiness: the 'dance of life' appears here as a purely mechanical and sometimes insubstantial activity, with no high aim and purpose. Whether it appears 'horrible', as Mahler believed it did, may be a matter of personal reaction; but undeniably, the sense of an apparently unstoppable nattering and nagging does become so strong in the end as to motivate the extraordinary revulsion which is the climax of the movement – the great outburst which Mahler described as 'a cry of disgust'. And the opening of the hymn-like movement for contralto solo, which follows this movement without a break, certainly comes as a welcome relief and an elevation to a higher plane.

So the 'programme' of the symphony resolves itself into a symbolic des-

cription of a psychological mood-sequence: a sense of outrage at the omnipotence of death, a haunting awareness of the fragility of life's happiness, and
a feeling of disgust at the mechanical and aimless triviality of everyday life,
followed by a turning away to faith in God and belief in resurrection and
eternal life.

Even so, we are still left with a nagging question. The 'call' which 'sounded
through' Mahler's life – the challenge to find some significance in a life which
is doomed to extinction – is one familiar to most of us, and we can find no
difficulty in responding to the feelings expressed in the first three movements.
But for the many of us who cannot answer this challenge by invoking the
Christian belief in immortality, what significance can there be in the culmination of the symphony – the part which presents the ostensible 'message' of
the work?

Strangely enough, it does have great significance for us, since a hearing of
it comes as a tremendous emotional experience. Yet the reason is clear. Music
cannot express intellectual concepts, but only feelings; and what we all respond to is the feelings of faith and inspiration in the music, whether or not
we are convinced by the concepts in the text which were the object of these
feelings. Mahler's affirmations are ultimately of faith and inspiration in life
itself, whether they arose, as in the Second, Third and Eighth Symphonies, from
the religious beliefs he held at the time, or as in *The Song of the Earth* and the
unfinished Tenth, from his realistic coming to terms with mortality when his
religious beliefs failed him. The 'Resurrection' Symphony raises us, not into
another world, but on to the plane of spiritual conflict and achievement where
life alone has value and significance.

*

The massive C minor sonata structure of the first movement has four con-
flicting elements: a funeral march of tragic grandeur; nostalgic pastoral
music; a mournful theme, introduced in the development; and moments of
latent triumph. The last includes a brass chorale which transmutes the 'Dies
Irae' into a bold, confident hymn, and eventually culminates in an affirmative
climax in E flat (foreshadowing the symphony's ultimate progression to that
key). But the funeral march rides ruthlessly over everything, ending the movement in exhausted resignation, and a spasm of horror.

The second movement is a Ländler in A flat – a single long stream of melody
which twice yields to a troubled trio, rising at times to the ferocity of the
funeral march, but returns to provide a tranquil ending. The 'image of a long-
dead hour of happiness' has succeeded at least temporarily in obliterating
the horror of death.

But then comes the harsh re-awakening to the confusion of life – a C minor
scherzo, in fast waltz-tempo, which views the futile dance of life in many
aspects: sinister, droll, joyful (the 'popular' first trio) and sentimental (the
trumpets' close harmony in the second); but the restless *moto perpetuo* of

the St Anthony song pervades everything, finally provoking a terrible protest (B flat minor chord over C) – the 'cry of disgust'. A sudden vision of peace descends (sustained wind chords and contented horn phrases); but it is soon dispelled by the *moto perpetuo*, which ends the movement in sardonically sinister mood.

Without pause, the contralto begins the fourth movement, the rapt, hymn-like setting, in D flat, of the *Wunderhorn* poem 'Urlicht'. This moving music, as Mahler said, 'throws a bright light on what has gone before. . . . The matinal voice of faith sounds in our ears: "I am from God, and to God will return." '

The finale breaks in immediately with the 'cry of disgust': 'We are confronted once more with terrifying questions'. This gigantic movement, moving from C major-minor to E flat, evokes the Last Judgement in a sequence of visionary scenes: it takes up material from the other movements (except the Ländler), especially the triumphant elements from the funeral march and the vision of peace from the scherzo. The 'cry of disgust' dies away into a profound calm – spacious horn phrases and a soft off-stage horn call. The 'Dies Irae' chorale enters quietly; it is answered by a solemn, assured trombone theme which generates confident horn fanfares. A supplicating cor anglais melody rises in anguished sequence; the chorale reappears, transmuted into affirmation, and the horn fanfares return with greater animation. Suddenly a ferocious march begins; but soon the chorale theme enters, transformed into a jaunty march, surmounted by an equally jaunty trumpet version of the solemn trombone theme heard earlier: 'the dead arise and stream on in endless procession'. The march eventually culminates in sheer terror – 'the cry for mercy and forgiveness strikes fearfully on our ears'; but it fades away, and the supplicating theme is heard again. Then another 'popular' march sounds off-stage, and against it the supplicating theme soars in agitated appeal on strings and wind. The climax is a last overpowering 'cry of disgust', and peace returns, as at first. Then comes the magical moment: the solemn last trumpet (horns and trumpets off-stage) mingled with liquid bird calls (flute and piccolo). Out of silence emerges the whispered chorus, in G flat: 'Rise again, yea, thou shalt rise again. . . . He who called thee will grant thee immortal life.' It gathers strength, and the symphony moves towards its majestic conclusion. The 'resurrection' theme is, characteristically, an ennobled form of the jaunty trumpet tune; the supplicating theme acquires words added to the text by Mahler himself – 'O believe, my heart . . . what thou hast lived for, fought for, will be thine . . . thou hast not lived in vain, suffered in vain.' Later, the soprano sings the 'Urlicht' melody 'I am from God and will return to God' to the words 'With wings which I have won me, I shall soar upwards'. After a mighty climax (resurrection theme in E flat), the original 'affirmative' music provides a broad peroration on orchestra and organ.

URLICHT

O Röschen rot!
Der Mensch liegt in grösster Not!
Der Mensch liegt in grösster Pein!
Je lieber möcht' ich im Himmel sein!

Da kam ich auf einen breiten Weg:
Da kam ein Engelein und wollt' mich
abweisen.
Ach nein! Ich liess mich nicht abweisen!
Ich bin von Gott und will wieder zu Gott!
Der liebe Gott wird mir ein Lichtchen geben,
Wird leuchten mir bis in das ewig selig
Leben!

(*from* Des Knaben Wunderhorn)

Auferstehn', ja auferstehn' wirst du,
Mein Staub, nach kurzer Ruh!
Unsterblich Leben! Unsterblich Leben
Wird der dich rief dir geben.

Wieder aufzublühn wirst du gesät!
Der Herr der Ernte geht
Und sammelt Garben
Uns ein, die starben!

O glaube, mein Herz, O glaube:
Es geht dir nichts verloren!
Dein ist, was du gesehnt!
Dein, was du geliebt,
Was du gestritten!

O glaube,
Du wardst nicht umsonst geboren!
Hast nicht umsonst gelebt,
Gelitten!

Was entstanden ist
Das muss vergehen!
Was vergangen, auferstehen!
Hör' auf zu beben!
Bereite dich zu leben!

O Schmerz! Du Alldurchdringer!
Dir bin ich entrungen!
O Tod! Du Allbezwinger!
Nun bist du bezwungen!

PRIMEVAL LIGHT

O red rose!
Man lies in deepest need,
Man lies in deepest Pain.
Yes, I would rather be in heaven!

I came upon a broad pathway:
An angel came and wanted to send me away.
Ah no! I would not be sent away!
I am from God and will return to God.
The dear God will give me a light,
Will light me to eternal blessed life!

Rise again, yea, thou shalt rise again,
My dust, after short rest!
Immortal life! Immortal life
He who called thee will grant thee.

To bloom again art thou sown!
The Lord of the Harvest goes
And gathers in, like sheaves,
Us who died.

O believe, my heart, O believe
Nothing is lost with thee!
Thine is what thou hast desired,
What thou hast lived for,
What thou hast fought for!

O believe,
Thou wert not born in vain!
Hast not lived in vain,
Suffered in vain!

What has come into being
Must perish,
What perished must rise again.
Cease from trembling!
Prepare thyself to live!

O Pain, thou piercer of all things,
From thee have I been wrested!
O Death, thou masterer of all things,
Now art thou mastered!

Mit Flügeln, die ich mir errungen,	*With wings which I have won me,*
In heissem Liebesstreben,	*in love's fierce striving,*
Werd' ich entschweben	*I shall soar upwards*
Zum Licht, zu dem kein Aug' gedrungen!	*To the light to which no eye has soared.*
Sterben werd' ich, um zu leben!	*I shall die, to live!*
Aufersteh'n, ja aufersteh'n	*Rise again, yea thou wilt rise again,*
Wirst du, mein Herz, in einem Nu!	*My heart, in the twinkling of an eye!*
Was du geschlagen	*What thou hast fought for*
Zu Gott wird es dich tragen!	*Shall lead thee to God!*

(*Klopstock/Mahler*)

SYMPHONY NO. 3 IN D, *for contralto, boys' and women's choirs and orchestra; composed 1895–6; first performed at Krefeld, 1902, under Mahler.*
This work was even more revolutionary than the Second Symphony; although the orchestra was slightly reduced (eight horns and four trumpets), the scale was larger (a hundred minutes), and there were six movements (the first lasting nearly forty minutes). Again Mahler used voices in two of the movements (the fourth and fifth), but the finale was purely instrumental.

*

Bruno Walter has left us an unforgettable pen-portrait of Mahler at the time when he had just completed his Second Symphony and would soon be starting his Third. The year was 1894: Walter, a youth of eighteen, had gone to Hamburg to try for the post of repetiteur at the Opera, where Mahler was chief conductor. He had read the scathing reviews of the recent Weimar performance of Mahler's First Symphony, denouncing it for 'sterility', 'triviality' and above all 'immoderation'. He had wanted to meet this 'immoderate' man, and now he found himself face to face with him:

> There he stood . . . thin, pale, slight of stature; the steep forehead of his long face framed in jet-black hair; his eyes full of meaning behind his glasses; lines of sadness and humour furrowing a countenance which revealed an amazing range of expressions as he spoke to anyone: as fascinating, demonic and intimidating an incarnation of Hoffmann's Kapellmeister Kreisler as could have presented itself to a youthful reader of that author. . . .

Kapellmeister Mahler certainly worked like a demon, during his six years at Hamburg, to improve the standard there; and he also introduced many new works, including Verdi's *Falstaff* and Puccini's *Manon Lescaut* (both completed as recently as 1892). All this activity so fully occupied the winter months that he was only able to compose during his summer vacations. Each

year, when the opera season was over, he retired to the Austrian countryside
– at this period to the village of Steinbach am Attersee in the Salzburg
Alps – to carry on his work as a composer; and it was there, during 1895 and
1896, that he composed his Third Symphony.

In Steinbach, Mahler had a little hut in the middle of a field, furnished
only with a piano, a table, an armchair and a sofa. Every morning he was
there at six o'clock; breakfast was brought at seven, and he worked on till
midday, or more often till three in the afternoon. Then, after lunch, he would
wander about the fields, or go for long tramps across the hills, working out
his musical ideas in his head. Occasionally he would find relaxation in enter-
taining a privileged visitor or two.

His retreat to the countryside was not merely due to his need for seclusion.
He was a passionate nature-lover – or rather, he felt himself absorbed by
nature: not only by the beautiful and the charming, but by the comical and
the grotesque, even by the alien, and above all by the awe-inspiring. His wife,
Alma, writing of a different summer retreat some twelve years later, described
a most unnerving experience:

> One day in the summer he came running down from his hut in a perspiration,
> scarcely able to breathe. At last he came out with it: it was the heat, the stillness,
> the Pan-ic horror. He was overcome by this feeling of the goat-god's frightful and
> vivid eye upon him in his solitude, and he had to take refuge in the house among
> human beings, and go on with his work there.

Scarcely credible – yet Mahler was a quite incredible human being. It was
this intense awareness of nature that was the inspiration of the Third Symphony.

When he had almost completed it, he wrote in a letter to the great dramatic
soprano Anna von Mildenburg:

> Just imagine a work of such magnitude that it actually mirrors the whole world –
> one is, so to speak, only an instrument, played on by the universe. . . . My symphony
> will be something the like of which the world has never yet heard! . . . In it the
> whole of nature finds a voice. . . . Some passages of it seem so uncanny to me that
> I can hardly recognize them as my own work. . . .

Indeed, so overwhelming was Mahler's inspiration that he felt almost as if
he were God, creating the universe. When Bruno Walter turned up at Steinbach, and stared in wonder at the magnificent mountain scenery, Mahler said
'You needn't stand staring at that – I've already composed it all!' And at the
rehearsals for the first performance of the work, in Krefeld six years later,
he walked over to his wife after the run-through of the first movement, and
laughingly quoted Genesis 1, 25: 'And he saw that it was good'!

If such an attitude seems alarmingly like megalomania, we might remember
Mahler's constant awareness of the impersonality of the force that was driving him. He did in fact feel like an instrument that was being played on by
some unknown power: as he said in another context, 'We do not compose;

we are composed. And if his intoxication with his own work seems laughable to those who regard this symphony as a great fuss about nothing, we may recall the effect it had on the young Schoenberg. After hearing the first Vienna performance in 1904, he wrote to Mahler, saying:

I think I have experienced your symphony. I felt the struggle for illusions; I felt the pain of one disillusioned; I saw the forces of evil and good contending; I saw a man in a torment of emotion exerting himself to gain inner harmony. I sensed a human being, a drama, *truth*, the most ruthless truth!

The striking fact here, however, is that Schoenberg's view of the inner meaning of the work was so different from Mahler's own. As in the case of the Second Symphony, we are faced with the question how far Mahler's own programme for the work actually explains what it is 'about', or has any real relevance for the listener.

What was it, exactly, that was eating Mahler during those two Austrian summers of 1895 and 1896? In letters to friends, written in August 1895, after he had fully sketched all the movements except the first, he outlined a comprehensive programme for the symphony, as follows:

THE JOYFUL KNOWLEDGE
A Summer Morning's Dream
    I   Summer marches in
  II What the meadow flowers tell me
 III What the creatures of the forest tell me
 IV What night tells me (mankind)
  V What the morning bells tell me (the angels)
 VI What love tells me
VII The heavenly life (what the child tells me)

The main title, 'The Joyful Knowledge' ('Die fröhliche Wissenschaft'), came from Nietzsche's book of the same name; and although the whole programme is hardly Nietzschean in the true sense – it has, as we shall see, eventual Christian connotations – the title was borrowed by Mahler to indicate a new-found optimism, or rather a kind of mystical revelation of the validity and purpose of existence.

The sub-title 'A Summer Morning's Dream' later became 'A Summer *Noon-day's* Dream'; this was after he had completed the work by composing the fantastic first movement. The idea of noonday brings to mind 'the heat, the stillness, the Pan-ic horror' of Alma Mahler's description; and in fact Mahler now dropped the title 'The Joyful Knowledge', and described the introduction to the work as 'Pan awakes'. (By this time also, the seventh movement had been excluded: it was in fact composed, but it was set aside, and became the finale, and seed, of the Fourth Symphony).

Mahler's clearest explanation of the idea behind this strange programme is to be found in a letter to Dr Richard Batka, written in February 1896. Already, before the completion of the symphony, the second movement

('What the meadow flowers tell me') had been performed several times, and Mahler complained of the misconception that would result from this:

That this little piece (more of an intermezzo in the whole thing) must create misunderstandings when detached from its connection with the complete work, my most significant and vastest creation, can't keep me from letting it be performed alone. I have no choice; if I want to be heard, I can't be too fussy, and so this modest little piece will doubtless . . . present me to the public as the 'sensuous', perfumed 'singer of nature'. – That this nature hides within itself everything that is frightful, great, and also lovely (which is exactly what I wanted to express in the entire work, in a sort of evolutionary development) – of course no one ever understands this. It always strikes me as odd that most people, when they speak of 'nature', think only of flowers, little birds, and woodsy smells. No one knows the god Dionysus, the great Pan. There now! You have a sort of programme – that is, a sample of how I make music. Everywhere and always, it is only the voice of nature! . . . Now it is the world, Nature in its totality, which is, so to speak, awakened from fathomless silence that it may ring and resound.

So the idea behind the work was a conception of existence in its totality. The vast first movement was to represent the summoning of Nature out of non-existence by the god Pan, symbolized by the emergence of summer out of the dead world of winter; and after this, the five shorter movements were to represent the 'stages of being' (as Mahler expressed it in another letter), from vegetable and animal life, through mankind and the angels, to the love of God. For the word 'love' in the title of the sixth movement was used in a Christian sense, as Mahler explained to Anna von Mildenburg:

It's a matter of a different kind of love from the one you imagine. The motto to this movement reads:

> Vater, sieh an die Wunden mein!
> Kein Wesen lass verloren sein!
> (*Father, see these wounds of mine!*
> *Let not be lost one creature of thine!*)

. . . I could almost call the movement 'What God tells me'. And truly in the sense that God can only be understood as love. And so my work is a musical poem embracing all stages of development in a step-wise ascent. It begins with inanimate nature and ascends to the love of God.

As in the case of the First and Second Symphonies, Mahler eventually discarded his programme, leaving the music to speak for itself; and this it can certainly do, whether one accepts the programme or not. No doubt those with as strong a pantheistic sense as Mahler possessed when he conceived it will find the programme full of meaning, but there will be others who, although they may admire the work itself, will regard the programme as ridiculous. And some may even feel that Mahler was actually expressing something different from what he imagined: as we have seen, Schoenberg felt it to be the expression of a tormented personal conflict. And Bruno Walter described the first movement as being concerned with a stark opposition between two irreconcilable opposites – what he called 'primordial inertia' and 'savage, lust-impelled creativeness'.

Although we cannot deny the pantheistic inspiration of the symphony, which is so clear from Mahler's letters, it has to be admitted that the work is not dependent on its programme. Those who have no pantheistic sense, or no mystical intuition of any kind, are not thereby debarred from responding to the content of the work. The fundamental meaning at the root of Mahler's 'existence-in-its-totality' programme is that the symphony is concerned with the creative spring of life, whatever that may be; with its struggle to overcome hindrances and barriers; with its delight in beauty, and even what is grotesque and ugly; with its 'intimations of immortality' and its aspiration to replace discord and hate with concord and love. Words, vague words, of course; and yet the vaguer the better, perhaps, if we are to try to hint at the inexplicable 'meaning' of this music, which delves so deeply into the source of life and feeling.

*

The first movement is the most original and flabbergasting thing Mahler ever conceived. To express the primeval force of nature burgeoning out of winter into summer, he built an outsize, proliferating sonata structure out of a plethora of 'primitive' material: a rugged F major – D minor march tune for unison horns, like a great summons to awake; deep soft brass chords, eloquent of hidden power; sullen D minor growls on trombones, like primordial inertia; bayings of horns, upsurgings of basses, shrieks on woodwind, subterranean rumblings of percussion, and gross, uncouth trombone themes, like monstrous prehistoric voices. In opposition appears murmurous pastoral music in D major (wind chords, trilling muted strings, solo violin) with shrill bird calls (piccolo 'fanfares', out of tempo). The final basic element, most extraordinary of all, is Mahler's 'popular' march style raised to a cosmic level: summer, approaching from afar, 'marches in' gaudily with thumping military band music, clad in a stark, blaring polyphony of fanfares and countermelodies. An awe-inspiring 'Pan-ic' climax ends this exposition. The enormous scale of the movement may be judged by the fact that, after the extended development (which culminates in a wild episode entitled 'The Mob') Mahler allowed himself to repeat virtually the entire exposition. But eventually the march music triumphs in its own key of F, with vociferous fanfares and rattling percussion.

The next four movements are much shorter. The 'flower' minuet in A, with its noisily chattering trio, uses the folk style and chamber scoring of the lighter *Wunderhorn* songs. This continues in the 'birds and beasts' movement, a lively scherzo in C minor. The quaint main material, with its captivating bird calls, is from the *Wunderhorn* song about the dead cuckoo ('Ablösung im Sommer'); the first trio is a rough, bounding affair, like young animals at play; the second a distant, long-drawn, deliberately sentimental post-horn tune with high shimmering strings, which evokes all the heat and romantic atmosphere of the Austrian summer. Near the end, a fierce outburst on an E flat minor chord seems to tear a veil aside, revealing the great god Pan himself. The fourth movement brings the questionings of humanity, in a D major Adagio setting of Nietzsche's 'Midnight Song', for contralto: 'The world is deep, and deeper than the day imagined. Deep is its grief, but joy is deeper still than heartache. Grief says "Die", but all joy seeks eternity.' The first movement's 'hidden power' music is used, and one of its savage trumpet cries is transformed into human yearning; the movement is one of the stillest things in all music, with its cry of a night bird (oboe glissando) and its long-held contralto notes backed by thirds on trombones echoed by piccolos. In the 'angels' movement, boys' and women's voices sing a carol-like F major setting of the *Wunderhorn* poem 'Three angels were singing a sweet song', to a bright accompaniment of wind, horns, harp and glockenspiel; the troubled middle section, adding lower strings, turns to thoughts of sin, repentance and forgiveness.

The extended orchestral Adagio finale, in D, hymning the love of God, alternates two groups: a long-drawn string theme, using the nineteenth-century religiose vein, but with compelling passion; and a counterpoint of motives pressing forward with a burning, painful longing. The music eventually reaches the same awe-inspiring climax as in the first movement; then the first group, beginning quietly, finally rises in the brass to a fortissimo apotheosis – 'Nature in its totality rings and resounds'.

O Mensch! Gib Acht!	*O Man, take heed!*
Was spricht die tiefe Mitternacht?	*What does the deep midnight say?*
Ich schlief! Aus tiefem Traum bin ich erwacht!	*I was asleep, from deep dreams I have awoken.*
Die Welt ist tief!	*The world is deep,*
Und tiefer, als der Tag gedacht!	*And deeper than the day imagined.*
Tief ist ihr Weh!	*Deep is its grief!*
Lust, tiefer noch als Herzeleid!	*Joy, deeper still than heartache!*
Weh spricht: Vergeh!	*Grief says: Die!*
Doch alle Lust will Ewigkeit!	*But all joy seeks eternity,*
Will tiefe, tiefe Ewigkeit.	*Seeks deep, deep eternity.*

(*Nietzsche*)

Es sungen drei Engel einen süssen Gesang;	*Three angels were singing a sweet song.*
Mit Freuden es selig in dem Himmel klang,	*In blissful joy it rang through heaven.*
Sie jauchzten fröhlich auch dabei,	*They shouted too for joy,*
Dass Petrus sei von Sünden frei.	*That Peter was set free from sin.*

Und als der Herr Jesus zu Tische sass,	*And as the Lord Jesus sat at table,*
Mit seinen zwölf Jüngern das Abendmahl ass,	*And ate the supper with his disciples,*
Da sprach der Herr Jesus: Was stehst du denn hier?	*Lord Jesus said: Why do you stand here?*
Wenn ich dich anseh', so weinest du mir!	*When I look at you, you weep at me.*

"Und sollt' ich nicht weinen, du gütiger Gott?	*'And should I not weep, thou bounteous God?*
Ich hab übertreten die zehn Gebot.	*I have broken the ten commandments.*
Ich gehe und weine ja bitterlich.	*I wander weeping bitterly,*
Ach komm' und erbarme dich über mich! "	*O come and have mercy on me!'*

Hast du denn übertreten die zehn Gebot,	*If you have broken the ten commandments,*
So fall auf die Knie und bete zu Gott!	*Then fall on your knees and pray to God.*
Liebe nur Gott in alle Zeit!	*Love only God all the time!*
So wirst du erlangen die himmlische Freud'.	*Thus will you gain heavenly joy.*

Die himmlische Freud' ist eine selige Stadt,	*Heavenly joy is a blessed city,*
Die himmlische Freud', die kein Ende mehr hat!	*Heavenly joy, that has no end!*
Die himmlische Freude war Petro bereit't,	*Heavenly joy was granted to Peter,*
Durch Jesum, und Allen zur Seligkeit.	*Through Jesus, and to all men for eternal bliss.*

(*from* Des Knaben Wunderhorn)

SYMPHONY NO. 4, *for orchestra with soprano solo; composed 1899–1901; first performed in Munich, 1901, under Mahler.*

This marks the end of the first period, to which it is linked by its *Wunderhorn* inspiration and vocal finale; but it foreshadows the second in rejecting the 'monumental' apparatus, approaching the purely orchestral symphony, and introducing a newly-clarified texture. The orchestra is much reduced; the scale moderate (fifty minutes); the form the normal four-movement one – sonata-allegro, scherzo and trio, adagio, and rondo.

*

The first reactions against romanticism came from some of the romantics themselves, and none was more unexpected or more significant than what could be called the 'neo-rococo' trend – the tendency to revive the archaic classical style of Haydn and Mozart as an alternative to the textural thickness and emotional intensity of the post-Wagnerian idiom. The earliest move in this direction may have been Tchaikovsky's *Rococo Variations* for cello and orchestra, but the trend fully established itself in the eighteen-nineties, in certain works, and parts of works, by Mahler and Richard Strauss. It might be regarded as a first, genial step in the direction of the eventual, far-from-genial 'neo-classicism' which dominated the musical scene between the two great wars of the twentieth century.

In Mahler's case – the Fourth Symphony – it meant a reduction of the huge Wagnerian orchestra, which Strauss was not prepared to consider until his *Ariadne auf Naxos* of 1912 (where he went much further than Mahler, however, using only thirty-six players). For the score of the Fourth, Mahler returned to normal nineteenth-century practice in having only triple woodwind, four horns and three trumpets, and looked back even further to the eighteenth century in having no trombones at all – for the only time in any of his symphonic works. This light orchestra might be thought the inevitable outcome of his previously evident tendency towards chamber-scoring, except that from the Fifth onwards the Wagnerian orchestra returned again, to be used as before for the heaviest possible climaxes as well as for extreme clarity in the many passages of chamber orchestration. The fact is that Mahler's reduced orchestra was part of the Fourth's 'neo-rococo' stylization, which is peculiar to this work alone (though it left its trace on such things as the finale of the Fifth, the trio of the scherzo of the Sixth, and the finale of the Seventh).

But Mahler was not, any more than Strauss, merely content to archaize. If the actual materials of the Fourth sometimes recall Haydn and Mozart (in the opening movement), Schubert (in the scherzo), and even the classical Beethoven (in the slow movement), they are developed in an entirely late-romantic way in the interest of expressing a personal vision.

What this vision is, the finale makes absolutely clear, being a setting for soprano solo of one of the longer poems from *Des Knaben Wunderhorn*, which describes a naïve picture of heavenly bliss as seen through the eyes of a child – an Austrian child of Catholic upbringing. This finale was in fact the starting-point of the whole work: it was, as we have seen, originally composed as early as 1892; it then became the seventh movement of the Third Symphony ('What the child tells me'). But Mahler eventually rejected it from the Third (probably because the mood rather duplicated the 'angels' movement of that work), and used it instead as the cornerstone of the Fourth. Thus, the first three movements of this neo-rococo 'pastoral symphony' were extrapolated, as it were, out of the folk vision of the movement intended as finale; and indeed certain sections of these movements are actually formed out of material from it.

✳

The symphony opens with the jingling phrase which is to be used as the refrain of the finale, to suggest the sleigh bells of a celestial sleigh-ride; and early on in the development section, a high flute gives out a gay tune, like a boy whistling, which, at the joyous climax of the movement is taken up as a

67

trumpet tune, to reveal itself as a premonition of the first phrase of the finale's opening theme. In the scherzo, the Ländler-like trio section is based on a folky clarinet tune which is a premonitory form of the whole main opening theme of the finale; while in the slow movement, the great climax (for which Mahler characteristically regretted the absence of the trombones) brings back the first movement's trumpet theme, ready for it to be shortly transformed into the opening of the finale.

Nevertheless, although these ideas were in fact *derived from* the material of the finale, they do, in the symphony, fulfil their true function of *foreshadowing* that movement. But it should not be supposed that in consequence the earlier movements are all pure gaiety and contentment: too much has been made of the 'untroubled' character of the Fourth Symphony, as opposed to Mahler's other works. The first movement is certainly a pastoral 'walk through the countryside' movement, but, as with its equivalent in the First Symphony, the gay jog-trot exposition yields to an equivocal development section in which clouds gather progressively until a nightmare climax is reached (immediately following on the gay trumpet theme); and out of the subsidence following the climax there emerges the bitter trumpet-call which is to begin the Fifth Symphony, as the grim preludial fanfare of the opening funeral march. Moreover, this collapse causes the music to peter out completely, just as the recapitulation is beginning: there is a silence before the violins pick up the carefree main theme casually, as though nothing had really happened at all. This amazing moment, one of Mahler's masterstrokes, pinpoints the strange character of the Fourth Symphony, which has been so misunderstood: it is not that there are no shadows in this work – on the contrary, there are some very dark ones – but they are seen, from out of this innocent pastoral world, as figures moving behind a veil, which obscures their naked horror, and makes them like the bogeymen who appear in illustrations to books of fairy-tales.

The jogging country dance which forms the scherzo was originally headed 'Freund Hein spielt auf' ('Friend Hein strikes up'). This character is a sinister figure in German folk-lore, an ostensibly friendly minstrel, like the Pied Piper, who leads his followers to the land of the 'Beyond'; he is clearly a symbol of death, who is so often represented as playing a violin: the title might be paraphrased as 'Death takes the fiddle'. The movement does, in fact, contain a prominent solo violin part for the leader of the orchestra, who is asked to tune his instrument up a whole tone, to make it sound like a village fiddle. It has often been pointed out that there is nothing gruesome about the movement itself; this is certainly true, but there is something 'Freund Hein-like' – disquieting – about the music, which should not be taken too much for granted at its 'Ländlerisch' face value. The main material is curiously wry, with its peaky violin solo, its often querulous obbligato horn part, and its weird solo counterpoints for wind and brass instruments on its later occurrences. But the trio sections, lazily cheerful in the style of the real Ländler, provide a happy contrast to the grotesque main scherzo, and thus they again veil, as it were, the disturbing spectres evoked by the music.

The slow movement opens with some of the most heart-easing music ever written by Mahler or anyone else – a transfigured cradle song. And yet this lullaby is no less equivocal than the two previous movements. The present writer, hearing this movement for the first time, found it bringing a line of Hardy irresistibly into his head – 'I seem where I was before my birth, and after death may be' – and was amazed to discover later that Mahler had actually written the movement under the inspiration of 'a vision of a tombstone on which was carved an image of the departed, with folded arms, in eternal sleep'. In opposition to this ineffable music emerges a strain of deep sadness – 'To sleep – perchance to dream?' – and the two ideas alternate in double variation form, until at last the vivid climax throws open the gates of paradise, ready for the finale. This climax has brought the movement into E major, a surprising key, except that it clinches the general sharpwards tendency of the whole work – the A major of the first movement's whistling flute tune, the D major of the swooning dance music that crowns the scherzo, the E major of the quickest variation of the slow movement itself, and now (after a return to G major) the movement's climax. So the backward-looking 'neo-rococo' style of the symphony meets and mingles with the forward-looking 'progressive tonality' of its key-sequence. For this sharpwards tendency of the first three movements is again an extrapolation (and a foreshadowing) of the finale, which itself moves from a gently happy G major towards an ecstatic transcendent E major, dying away blissfully in that key with the faint thrumming of a harp.

DAS HIMMLISCHE LEBEN

Wir geniessen die himmlischen Freuden,
D'rum tun wir das Irdische meiden.
Kein weltlich' Getümmel
Hört man nicht im Himmel!
Lebt Alles in sanftester Ruh'!

Wir führen ein englisches Leben!
Sind dennoch ganz lustig daneben!
Wir tanzen und springen,
Wir hüpfen und singen!
Sankt Peter im Himmel sieht zu!

Johannes das Lämmlein auslasset,
Der Metzger Herodes drauf passet!
Wie führen ein geduldig's,
Unschuldig's, geduldig's,
Ein liebliches Lämmlein zu Tod!

HEAVENLY LIFE

We revel in heavenly pleasures,
Leaving all that is earthly behind us.
No worldly turmoil
Is heard in heaven;
We all live in sweetest peace.

We lead an angelic existence,
And so we are perfectly happy.
We dance and leap,
And skip and sing;
Saint Peter in Heaven looks on.

Saint John has lost his lambkin,
And butcher Herod is lurking:
We lead a patient,
Guiltless, patient,
Darling lambkin to death.

Sankt Lukas den Ochsen tät schlachten	*Saint Luke is slaying the oxen,*
Ohn' einig's Bedenken und Achten;	*Without the least hesitation;*
Der Wein kost't kein Heller	*Wine costs not a farthing*
Im himmlischen Keller;	*In the Heavenly tavern;*
Die Englein, die backen das Brot.	*The angels bake the bread.*
Gut' Kräuter von allerhand Arten,	*Fine sprouts of every description,*
Die wachsen im himmlischen Garten!	*Are growing in Heaven's garden.*
Gut' Spargel, Fisolen,	*Fine asparagus, fine herbs,*
Und was wir nur wollen,	*And all we desire,*
Ganze Schüsseln voll sind uns bereit!	*Huge platefuls for us are prepared.*
Gut' Äpfel, gut' Birn' und gut Trauben!	*Fine apples, fine pears and fine grapes,*
Die Gärtner, die alles erlauben!	*The gardeners let us pick freely.*
Willst Rehbock, willst Hasen?	*You want venison, hare?*
Auf offener Strassen	*In the open streets*
Sie laufen herbei!	*They go running around.*
Sollt' ein Festtag etwa kommen,	*And when there's a holiday near,*
Alle Fische gleich mit Freuden	*All the fishes come joyfully*
angeschwommen!	*swimming;*
Dort läuft schon Sankt Peter	*And off runs Saint Peter*
Mit Netz und mit Köder,	*With net and with bait,*
Zum himmlischen Weiher hinein.	*Towards the celestial pond.*
Sankt Martha die Köchin muss sein!	*Saint Martha will have to be cook!*
Kein Musik ist ja nicht auf Erden,	*There's no music at all on the earth*
Die unsrer verglichen kann werden.	*Which can ever compare with ours.*
Elftausend Jungfrauen	*Eleven thousand virgins*
Zu tanzen sich trauen!	*Are set dancing.*
Sankt Ursula selbst dazu lacht!	*Saint Ursula herself laughs to see it!*
Cäcilia mit ihren Verwandten	*Saint Cecilia with her companions*
Sind treffliche Hofmusikanten!	*Are splendid court musicians.*
Die englischen Stimmen	*The angelic voices*
Ermuntern die Sinnen!	*Delight the senses,*
Dass Alles für Freuden erwacht.	*For all things awake to joy.*

(*from* Des Knaben Wunderhorn)

MIDDLE PERIOD

The middle-period symphonies, Nos. 5 to 7, differ markedly from their predecessors. Gone are the folk inspiration, the explicit programmes, the fairytale elements, the song materials, the voices; instead we have a triptych of 'pure' orchestral works, more realistically rooted in human life, more stern and forthright of utterance, more tautly symphonic, with a new granite-like hardness of orchestration. But the songs must be examined first, since they had a considerable influence on the thematic style of the symphonies.

'REVELGE' AND 'DER TAMBOURSG'SELL', *two orchestral songs (1899 and 1901)*.

These last two *Wunderhorn* settings are as masterly as the preceding ten, but more powerful in style: stern military marches with heavy military percussion. 'Revelge' is a macabre quick march for an orchestra without trombones: it tells, with a sinister 'tralali, tralaley, tralalera' refrain, of a regiment returning from battle in the early morning, to hold their last parade in the village street – rank upon rank of grinning skeletons. 'Der Tamboursg'sell', a bitter funeral march, presents the last thoughts of a drummer-boy before his execution as a deserter: his dread of the gallows, his regimental pride, and his heart-broken farewell to his comrades.

REVELGE

Des Morgens zwischen drei'n und vieren,
da müssen wir Soldaten marschieren
das Gässlein auf und ab.
Tralali, tralaley, tralalera,
mein Schätzel sieht herab!

"Ach, Bruder, jetzt bin ich geschossen,
die Kugel hat mich schwere, schwer
  getroffen,
trag' mich in mein' Quartier!
Tralali, tralaley, tralalera,
es ist nicht weit von hier!"

"Ach, Bruder, ach, Bruder, ich kann dich
  nicht tragen,
die Feinde haben uns geschlagen!
helf' dir der liebe Gott,
helf' dir der liebe Gott!
Tralali, tralaley, tralalera,
ich muss, ich muss marschieren bis in Tod!"

"Ach, Brüder, ach, Brüder, ihr geht ja mir
  vorüber,
als wär's mit mir vorbei,
als wär's mit mir vorbei!
Tralali, tralaley, tralalera,
ihr tretet mir zu nah,
ihr tretet mir zu nah!

Ich muss wohl meine Trommel rühren,
ich muss meine Trommel wohl rühren,
tralali, tralaley, tralali, tralaley,
sonst werd' ich mich verlieren,
tralali, tralaley, tralala!"
Die Brüder, dick gesät, die Brüder, dick
  gesät,
sie liegen wie gemäht.

Er schlägt die Trommel auf und nieder,
er wecket seine stillen Brüder,
tralali, tralaley, tralali, tralaley,
sie schlagen und sie schlagen ihren Feind,
  Feind, Feind,
tralali, tralaley, tralalera,
ein Schrecken schlägt den Feind,
ein Schrecken schlägt den Feind!

Er schlägt die Trommel auf und nieder,

REVEILLE

From three to four o'clock every morning,
we soldiers must parade and go marching
along the village street.
Tralalee, tralalay, tralalaira,
my love looks down on me!

'O comrade, they've hit me, I'm wounded,
the bullet struck me, fair and square it
  struck me,
O help me back to base!
Tralalee, tralalay, tralalaira,
it's not so far from here!'

'O comrade, O comrade, I can't stop to help
you
our foes have struck, and we are beaten,
commend your soul to God,
commend your soul to God!
Tralalee, tralalay, tralalaira,
I must, I must march on to meet my death!'

'O comrades, O comrades, you pass me by
  so quickly,
As if I were a corpse,
as if I were a corpse!
Tralalee, tralalay, tralalaira,
you press on me too close,
you press on me too close!

My drum I now must start a-beating,
my drum I must now start a-beating,
tralalee, tralalay, tralalee, tralalay,
or I'll be lost for ever,
tralalee, tralalay, tralala!'
The comrades strewn so thick, the comrades
  strewn so thick,
seem mown down by a scythe.

He marches up and down a-drumming,
he wakens up his silent comrades,
tralalee, tralalay, tralalee, tralalay,
they fall upon the foe, upon the foe, foe, foe,
tralalee, tralalay, tralalaira,
and terror strikes the foe,
and terror strikes the foe!

He marches up and down a-drumming,

da sind sie vor dem Nachtquartier schon
  wieder,
tralali, tralaley, tralali, tralaley!
Ins Gässlein hell hinaus, hell hinaus,
sie zieh'n vor Schätzleins Haus,
tralali, tralaley, tralali, tralaley, tralalera,
sie zieh'n vor Schätzleins Haus, tralali!

Des Morgens stehen da die Gebeine,
in Reih' und Glied, sie steh'n wie
  Leichensteine,
in Reih' in Reih' und Glied.
Die Trommel steht voran, die Trommel steht
  voran,
dass sie ihn sehen kann!
Tralali, tralaley, tralali, tralaley, tralalera,
dass sie ihn sehen kann!

he leads them back towards their village
  quarters,
tralalee, tralalay, tralalee, tralalay!
In the street, so clear to see, clear to see,
they pass his sweetheart's house,
tralalee, tralalay, tralalee, tralalay,
  tralalaira,
they pass his sweetheart's house, tralalee!

Their bones are on parade in the morning,
in rank and file their skeletons are standing,
in rank, in rank and file.
The drummer's out in front, the drummer's
  out in front,
that she may see him there!
Tralalee, tralalay, tralalee, tralalay,
  tralalaira,
that she may see him there!

DER TAMBOURSG'SELL

Ich armer Tamboursg'sell!
Man führt mich aus dem G'wölb',
man führt mich aus dem G'wölb'!
Wär ich ein Tambour blieben,
dürft ich nicht gefangen liegen!

O Galgen, du hohes Haus,
du siehst so furchtbar aus!
Ich schau dich nicht mehr an!
Ich schau dich nicht mehr an,
weil i weiss, dass i g'hör d'ran,
weil i weiss, dass i g'hör d'ran!

Wenn Soldaten vorbeimarschier'n,
bei mir nit einquartier'n,
wenn sie fragen, wer i g'wesen bin:
"Tambour von der Leibkompanie,
Tambour von der Leibkompanie!"

Gute Nacht, ihr Marmelstein',
ihr Berg' und Hügelein!
Gute Nacht, ihr Offizier,
Korporal und Musketier!
Gute Nacht! Gute Nacht! Ihr Offizier,
Korporal und Grenadier!

THE DRUMMER-BOY

Woe's me, poor drummer-boy!
They lead me from the jail,
they lead me from the jail!
Had I remained a drummer,
then I'd not have been in prison!

O gallows, you high-built house,
how grim you seem to me!
I'll look at you no more,
I'll look at you no more,
for I know you're meant for me,
for I know you're meant for me!

When the soldiers come marching by,
who were not mates of mine,
when they ask, where and what I've been:
'Drummer-boy to the King's Bodyguard,
Drummer-boy to the King's Bodyguard!'

Good night, you marble rocks,
you mountains and little hills!
Good night, you officers,
corporals and musketeers!
Good night! Good night! You officers,
corporals and grenadiers!

Ich schrei' mit heller Stimm':	*I cry now, loud and clear:*
von euch ich Urlaub nimm!	*I take my leave of you,*
Von euch ich Urlaub nimm!	*I take my leave of you!*
Gute Nacht! Gute Nacht!	*Good night! Good night!*

FÜNF LIEDER NACH RÜCKERT, *five Rückert songs with orchestra* (*1901–2*); *later published with 'Revelge' and 'Der Tamboursg'sell'* as Sieben Lieder aus letzter Zeit (Seven Last Songs).

With one exception, they are in lyrical Lied style – Mahler's first real Lieder since 'Erinnerung'. The songs do not form a cycle, having no inner connection of mood, and Mahler used a different orchestra for each.

'Ich atmet' einen linden Duft', for single wind (two bassoons), three horns, harp, celesta, violins and violas, weaves a delicate tracery of summery murmurings around a poem praising the scent of the lime-tree; the point of the poem is the untranslatable play on the words *lind*, meaning 'delicate', and *Linde*, meaning 'lime-tree'.

For 'Blicke mir nicht in die Lieder' Mahler used an orchestra of single woodwind, one horn, harp, and strings without basses. It is the least inspired song of his maturity – a quaint setting of a rather arch lyric.

'Ich bin der Welt abhanden gekommen' is scored for oboe, cor anglais, two clarinets, two bassoons, two horns, harp and strings. It is Mahler's finest Lied: touching on the rich style of Strauss, it voices the familiar late-romantic mood of withdrawal from the world – new to Mahler, and treated with a depth and nobility characteristic of him.

'Um Mitternacht' is for full woodwind, horns and brass, with timpani, harp and piano, but without any strings. No Lied, but an extended symphonic-contrapuntal movement of austere grandeur, it opens with lonely night-thoughts of man's dark fate (bare wind counterpoints, with a stylized bird cry for oboe d'amore) and ends with triumphant reliance on the will of God (transformation of the 'lonely' material into a brief but potent brass chorale).

'Liebst du um Schönheit', scored (by Max Puttman, not Mahler) for woodwind without flutes, four horns, harp and strings, is a deeply-felt but delicate Lied, related to Strauss. It is Mahler's only personal love song, written for his wife: 'If you love me for beauty, youth, or riches, don't love me; if you love me for love, love me for ever.'

ICH ATMET' EINEN LINDEN DUFT

Ich atmet' einen linden Duft!	*I breathed a delicate fragrance.*
Im Zimmer stand ein Zweig der Linde,	*In the room stood a spray of lime,*

ein Angebinde von lieber Hand.
Wie lieblich war der Lindenduft!

a token from a beloved hand.
How lovely was the fragrance of lime!

Wie lieblich ist der Lindenduft,
das Lindenreis brachst du gelinde!
Ich atme leis im Duft der Linde –
der Liebe linden Duft.

How lovely is the fragrance of lime,
the spray of lime you delicately plucked!
I gently breathe the fragrance of lime –
the delicate fragrance of love.

BLICKE MIR NICHT IN DIE LIEDER

Blicke mir nicht in die Lieder!
Meine Augen schlag' ich nieder,
wie ertappt auf böser Tat.
Selber darf ich nicht getrauen,
ihrem Wachsen zuzuschauen.
Blicke mir nicht in die Lieder!
Deine Neugier ist Verrat!

Do not look into my songs;
I cast down my eyes,
as if surprised in a naughty deed.
I dare not even trust myself
to watch them growing.
Do not look into my songs;
your inquisitiveness is treason!

Bienen, wenn sie Zellen bauen,
lassen auch nicht zu sich schauen,
schauen selbst auch nicht zu.
Wenn die reichen Honigwaben
sie zu Tag befördet haben,
dann vor allen nasche du!

Bees, when they build cells,
also will not let themselves be watched,
and do not even watch themselves.
When the rich honeycombs
are at last brought to the light of day,
you shall be the first to taste!

ICH BIN DER WELT ABHANDEN GEKOMMEN

Ich bin der Welt abhanden gekommen,
mit der ich sonst viele Zeit verdorben;
sie hat so lange nichts von mir vernommen,
sie mag wohl glauben, ich sei gestorben!

I am lost to the world,
on which I squandered so much time;
it has for so long known nothing of me,
it may well believe that I am dead!

Es ist mir auch gar nichts daran gelegen,
ob sie mich für gestorben hält.
Ich kann auch gar nichts sagen dagegen,
denn wirklich bin ich gestorben der Welt.

Not that I am in any way concerned
if it takes me for dead;
nor can I really deny it,
for truly I am dead to the world.

Ich bin gestorben dem Weltgetümmel
und ruh' in einem stillen Gebiet!
Ich leb' allein in meinem Himmel,
in meinem Lieben, in meinem Lied.

I am dead to the world's commotion
and at peace in a still land!
I live alone in my own heaven,
in my love, in my song.

UM MITTERNACHT

Um Mitternacht hab' ich gewacht und aufgeblickt zum Himmel; kein Stern vom Sterngewimmel hat mir gelacht um Mitternacht.	*At midnight* *I kept watch* *and looked up to heaven;* *no star of all the host of stars* *smiled on me* *at midnight.*

Um Mitternacht
hab' ich gedacht
hinaus in dunkle Schranken;
es hat kein Lichtgedanken
mir Trost gebracht
um Mitternacht.

At midnight
I sent my thoughts
far to the bounds of dark space;
no vision of light
brought me comfort
at midnight.

Um Mitternacht
kämpft' ich die Schlacht,
die Schläge meines Herzens;
ein einz'ger Puls des Schmerzens
war angefacht
um Mitternacht.

At midnight
I took note of
the beating of my heart;
a single pulse of sorrow
was set in motion
at midnight.

Um Mitternacht
kämpft' ich die Schlacht,
O Menschheit, deiner Leiden;
nicht konnt' ich sie entscheiden
mit meiner Macht
um Mitternacht.

At midnight
I fought the battle,
O Mankind, of your sufferings;
I could not gain the victory
by my own strength
at midnight.

Um Mitternacht
hab' ich die Macht
in deine Hand gegeben!
Herr über Tod und Leben:
Du hältst die Wacht
um Mitternacht!

At midnight
I gave my strength
into Thy hands!
Lord of death and life,
thou keep'st the watch
at midnight!

LIEBST DU UM SCHÖNHEIT

Liebst du um Schönheit,
O nicht mich liebe!
Liebe die Sonne,
sie trägt ein gold'nes Haar!

If you love for beauty,
then do not love me!
love the Sun,
for he has golden hair.

Liebst du um Jugend,
O nicht mich liebe!
Liebe den Frühling,
der jung ist jedes Jahr!

If you love for youth,
then do not love me!
love the Spring,
which is young every year.

Liebst du um Schätze,	*If you love for riches,*
O nicht mich liebe!	*then do not love me!*
Liebe die Meerfrau,	*love a mermaid,*
sie hat viel Perlen klar!	*for she has many fine pearls!*
Liebst du um Liebe,	*If you love for love,*
O ja mich liebe!	*then yes, do love me!*
Liebe mich immer,	*love me for ever,*
dich lieb' ich immerdar!	*I'll love you evermore!*

KINDERTOTENLIEDER (SONGS ON THE DEATHS OF CHILDREN), *a cycle of five orchestral songs (1901–4).*

The poems were written by Friedrich Rückert out of grief for his two children who had died, presumably of diphtheria; three years after Mahler completed his cycle, one of his own children died. But suggestions of clairvoyance are unnecessary; he began the work before his marriage, possibly impelled by the name of Rückert's little boy – Ernst.

The folk element has vanished, and the lyrical Lied style is now handled in his own symphonic-contrapuntal way. The orchestra is small – no brass, two horns, double wind (four horns and triple wind in the last song); the chamber orchestration is of a new, rarified kind anticipating *The Song of the Earth* – solitary instrumental voices moving in bare counterpoints; the style is Mahler's own distillation of late-romantic idioms – by turns emotionally stunned, wildly grief-stricken, warmly affectionate, and radiantly consolatory. The first four songs present: (1) the sunrise that brings no comfort; (2) memories of the children's star-like eyes; (3) habitual actions that evoke too vivid memories; (4) a vision that the children have only wandered away into another world, where their parents will one day find them again. The last song describes the storm that raged on the day of the funeral, the violent grief of the heart-broken father, and finally the peace and haven the children have found in spite of the storm – a haven of eternal sleep rather than the paradise of the Fourth Symphony. The nihilism of the Sixth Symphony had intervened before the song was composed.

1

Nun will die Sonn' so hell aufgeh'n,	*Now will the sun as brightly rise*
als sei kein Unglück, die Nacht gescheh'n!	*As though no evil befell last night!*
Das Unglück geschah nur mir allein!	*The evil befell just me alone;*
die Sonne, sie scheinet allgemein!	*The sun, it shines on all mankind!*

Du musst nicht die Nacht in dir
  verschränken;
musst sie ins ew'ge Licht versenken!

You must not enfold the night within you;
You must immerse it in eternal light!

Ein Lämplein verlosch in meinem Zelt!
Heil sei dem Freudenlicht der Welt!

A lamp has gone out in my abode;
Hail to the whole world's gladdening light!

2

Nun seh' ich wohl, warum so dunkle
  Flammen
ihr sprühet mir in manchem Augenblicke.
– O Augen! – Gleichsam, um voll in einem
  Blicke
zu drängen eure ganze Macht zusammen.

Now I see clearly, O eyes, why such dark
* flames*
So often leapt out at me
As if you wanted to concentrate
The whole sum of your strength in a
* single look.*

Doch ahn't ich nicht, weil Nebel mich
  umschwammen,
gewoben vom verblendenden Geschicke,
dass sich der Strahl bereits zur Heimkehr
  schicke,
dorthin, von wannen alle Strahlen stammen.

Yet I never suspected (because of the mists
* that hovered round me,*
All spun by the deceitful loom of fate),
That those bright beams already sought to
* journey*
Back home – to the place where every
* beam originates.*

Ihr wolltet mir mit eurem Leuchten sagen:
Wir möchten nah dir bleiben gerne,
doch ist uns das vom Schicksal
  abgeschlagen.
Sieh' uns nur an, denn bald sind wir dir
  ferne!

You wanted with your shining light to tell
* me:*
'We'd dearly love to stay here by you,
But this our destiny denies us.
Ah look at us, for soon we'll be far from you!

Was dir nur Augen sind in diesen Tagen:
in künft'gen Nächten sind es dir nur Sterne.

What are but eyes to you, these present
* days,*
In nights to come will be to you but stars.'

3

Wenn dein Mütterlein
tritt zur Tür herein,
und den Kopf ich drehe,
ihr entgegen sehe,
fällt auf ihr Gesicht
erst der Blick mir nicht,
sondern auf die Stelle,
näher nach der Schwelle,
dort, wo würde dein
lieb' Gesichtchen sein,
wenn du freudenhelle
trätest mit herein,
wie sonst, mein Töchterlein!

When your mother dear
Comes in through the door,
And I turn my head,
To look across at her,
'Tis not on her face
That my glance falls first,
But upon that place,
Nearer to the floor,
There, where your dear face
Always used to be,
When all bright with joy
You would come in with her,
In bygone days, my daughter dear!

Wenn dein Mütterlein
tritt zur Tür herein
mit der Kerze Schimmer,
ist es mir, als immer
kämst du mit herein,
huschtest hinterdrein,
als wie sonst ins Zimmer!
O du, des Vaters Zelle,
ach, zu schnell, zu schnelle
erlosch'ner Freudenschein!

When your dear mother
Comes in through the door
In her candle's shimmer,
It's as though you always
Came in with her too,
Toddling after her,
As you used to do.
O you, your father's flesh and blood,
Ah, gladdening light
Too swiftly extinguished!

4

Oft denk' ich, sie sind nur ausgegangen!
Bald werden sie wieder nach Hause gelangen.
Der Tag ist schön! O sei nicht bang!
Sie machen nur einen weiten Gang.

How often I think they're just out walking;
They won't be much longer, they'll soon be
*   returning.*
The day is fine, O never fear!
They're only taking the long way back.

Jawohl, sie sind nur ausgegangen
und werden jetzt nach Hause gelangen.
O, sei nicht bang, der Tag ist schön!
Sie machen nur den Gang zu jenen Höh'n!

Oh yes, they've only gone out walking,
And even now they must be returning.
O never fear, the day is fine!
They're only taking the path into the hills!

Sie sind uns nur vorausgegangen
und werden nicht wieder nach Haus
    verlangen!
Wir holen sie ein auf jenen Höh'n
im Sonnenschein! Der Tag ist schön
auf jenen Höh'n!

They've only started out before us
And won't come back home at all!
We'll soon overtake them, up on the hills,
In the sunshine! the day is fine
Upon the hills!

5

In diesem Wetter, in diesem Braus,
nie hätt'ich gelassen die Kinder hinaus,
Man hat sie hinaus getragen.
Ich durfte nichts dazu sagen.

In this grim weather, this raging storm,
I'd never have sent the children outside!
But out of the house they've borne them.
I had no say in the matter.

In diesem Wetter, in diesem Saus,
nie hätt 'ich gelassen die Kinder hinaus,
ich fürchtete, sie erkranken;
das sind nun eitle Gedanken.

In this grim weather, this howling gale,
I'd never have let the children outside,
I'd fear they might catch an illness;
Now these are but idle thoughts

In diesem Wetter, in diesem Graus,
nie hätt' ich gelassen die Kinder hinaus.

In this grim weather, this dreadful blast,
I'd never have dared let the children
*   outside.*

Ich sorgte, sie stürben morgen,	*I'd fear they might die tomorrow;*
das ist nun nicht zu besorgen.	*Now this is no cause for worry.*

In diesem Wetter, in diesem Graus!	*In this grim weather, this raging storm,*
nie hätt' ich gesendet die Kinder hinaus.	*I'd never have dared send the children*
Man hat sie hinaus getragen;	*outside!*
ich durfte nichts dazu sagen!	*But out of the house they've borne them;*
	I had no say in the matter!

In diesem Wetter, in diesem Saus,	*In this grim weather, this howling gale,*
in diesem Braus,	*This raging storm,*
sie ruh'n, als wie in der Mutter Haus.	*They rest, as if in their mother's house.*
Von keinem Sturm erschrecket,	*No storm can now frighten them,*
von Gottes Hand bedecket,	*The hand of God protects them,*
sie ruh'n wie in der Mutter Haus!	*They rest as if in their mother's house!*

SYMPHONY NO. 5, *composed 1901–2; first performed at Cologne, 1904, under Mahler.*

Here he took the decisive step of returning to the purely orchestral symphony foreshadowed in the Fourth, but he now modified and expanded it. The orchestra is a full one, with six horns and four trumpets; the time-scale large (seventy minutes); there are five movements, and only after the first two (neither of them a sonata-allegro) do we encounter the traditional formal plan.

*

Aaron Copland has said that 'The difference between Beethoven and Mahler is the difference between watching a great man walk down the street and watching a great actor play the part of a great man walking down the street'. It is easy to see what Copland is driving at – the manifest element of impersonation in much of Mahler's music – but he does not go deep enough to explain why this should be. There is nothing superficial or insincere about Mahler, but only an underlying psychological instability. The real difference between Beethoven and him is that between watching a great man walk down a street in which he feels himself secure, and is therefore perfectly at ease with his greatness, and watching a great man walk down a street in which he feels himself totally insecure, and is therefore obliged to act out his greatness, self-consciously and defiantly – because he is scarcely able to credit it in his heart of hearts, uncertain whether the street will not suddenly cease to be a reassuring background and become hostile territory in which he will be an outcast.

Mahler had to walk down so many streets, and felt at home in none of them; and this is the fundamental origin of the almost disruptive contrasts in his music. With each new symphony – and sometimes with each new movement inside a symphony – we are taken into a different world. In each case there is a passionate, even desperate identification with a certain attitude – but only, in the last resort, for what it is worth; suddenly the scene changes, and another attitude is being identified with – but again only for what it is worth. In the first four symphonies we find Mahler striving to identify himself with four different kinds of idealism: the power of the will against fate in the First, the Christian belief in resurrection in the Second, a dionysiac pantheism based on Nietzsche in the Third, the indestructibility of innocence in the Fourth. Into all these symphonies the youthful lyricism of Mahler's early songs enters, either in instrumental arrangements or else actually sung by voices – the voices of children, or of adults possessed of a childlike, trusting faith.

None of these idealistic worlds proved a haven to rest in, and the Fifth Symphony, completed in 1902 at the age of forty-two, brought a more than usually determined wiping of the slate. It marks the beginning of Mahler's full maturity, being the first of a trilogy of 'realistic', purely instrumental symphonies – Nos. 5, 6, and 7 – which occupied him during his middle period. The programmes, the voices, the songs, and the movements based on songs have gone; and the delicate or warm harmonic sonorities which formerly brought relief from pain have been largely replaced by a new type of naked contrapuntal texture, already foreshadowed in parts of the Fourth **Symphony**, but now given a hard edge by the starkest possible use of the **woodwind and** brass.

*

In the Fifth Symphony, although it has no actual programme, there are two manifest and utterly opposed attitudes which are set side by side, with so little reconciliation between them as to threaten the work with disunity. The symphony might almost be described as schizophrenic, in that the most tragic and the most joyful worlds of feeling are separated off from one another, and only bound together by Mahler's unmistakable command of large-scale symphonic construction and unification.

The symphony progresses tonally from C sharp minor to D major, and the five movements are sub-divided into three parts. The first part consists of the two opening movements: linked emotionally and thematically, they explore to the full the tragic view of life, and give only a late and fleeting glimpse of the opposite view – that of triumphant life-affirmation. The first movement is a black funeral march in C sharp minor, beginning with a hollow trumpet fanfare in the minor mode, which is to strike in at various points as a kind of refrain – brooding or ferocious according to the general mood. This beginning stems from a passage in the Fourth Symphony, as though Mahler wanted to preserve at least a thread of continuity between his new 'realistic' world and the world of naïve innocence he had just left behind. The main theme of the first movement is a long-drawn string threnody (related melodically to 'Der Tamboursg'sell' and the first of the *Kindertotenlieder*) with a pathetic contrasting strain in A flat for wind. The trio section is a terrible storm of grief in B flat minor – a bitter cry on the trumpet surmounted by a wild headlong torrent of notes on violins; a broad major theme, rising hopefully on violins, is soon submerged. After the reprise of the march, the trio returns, slowed down to the march's tempo and mood, and a new, anguished figure is heard (a rising minor ninth falling to the octave), which will permeate the next movement (it is in that movement's key, A minor). After a fiercely lamenting climax, the trumpet call ends the movement *pianissimo*, in desolation.

The A minor Allegro second movement is frenetic, and it reverses the situation of the first: the ferocious mood of protest is basic, and there are slower sections which are related to the funeral march music of the first movement – not only in mood, but in some of the actual thematic material. The first section, demonic and hysterical in character (but combated by the first movement's 'hopeful' theme), alternates over long periods with a slow, sorrowful march melody. Each occurs three times, ever more varied in treatment and shorter in span; then appears the jaunty march and the shout of triumph mentioned earlier in this book as an example of the Whole Truth (see p. 16). But the attempt to exult is premature; the main material resumes, followed once more by the slow march. Eventually, however, the shout of triumph breaks through again (as before, in D – the key that will dominate the rest of the symphony), to become a noble brass chorale. Then it fades with the swiftness of a dream; the main material returns for the last time, to end the movement in a deathly whisper. What is to follow will contradict the despairing mood of Part I entirely.

Part II consists of the third movement only – the big scherzo – and the moment it begins, the schizophrenic character of the work emerges. It completely contradicts the nihilistic mood and minor tonality of practically everything that has gone before, by switching to the brilliant key of D major, and to an exploration of the joyfully affirmative view of life, both of which are to occupy the rest of the symphony. Thus the dark world of Part I is not gradually dispelled by a process of spiritual development: it is abruptly rejected in favour of a completely different attitude. The tragic view of life is one way of looking at things, the symphony seems to say, and this is another: the two different attitudes are always there, and either or both may be right – but it is impossible to reconcile them.

This scherzo is a symphonic Ländler, with an ebullient obbligato part for the first horn player of the orchestra. Admittedly, the waltz-like trio section brings a mood of nostalgia; and there is an awesome climax with horns echoing and re-echoing as if across mountain distances, which leads to haunting music full of sadness and loneliness. But these passages have nothing emotionally in common with the despairing laments of the first part of the work; and in any case, they are subsidiary to the excited Ländler music, which returns all the time, in rondo fashion, and eventually brings the movement to a jubilant ending. The scherzo is really a dance of life, evoking all the bustle of a vital existence, as opposed to the concentration on the inevitability of death in the funeral marches and ferocious protests of Part 1; and if the scherzo of the Second Symphony views the dance of death as essentially senseless and futile, it is seen here as fundamentally thrilling and exhilarating.

The third and final part of the symphony consists of the last two movements. First comes the famous Adagietto for strings and harp only, which is a quiet haven of peace in F major between the strenuous activity of the D major scherzo and the equally strenuous activity of the D major finale. Pervaded with the familiar romantic mood of withdrawal from the strain and tension of life into the quietude of the inner self, the Adagietto has much in common with Mahler's great song 'Ich bin der Welt abhanden gekommen' ('I am lost to the world'), which ends with the words 'I live alone, in my own heaven, in my love, in my singing'.

Out of this movement's quiet retreat, the finale emerges immediately – and magically. Solo wind and horn present a few short folk-like motives, from which the movement is to grow (a last glance at the *Wunderhorn* world – the bassoon actually has a figure from the song 'Lob des hohen Verstandes'). The horns take up one of the motives as the main rondo theme, over a pastoral drone-bass. The mood is again joyful and exuberant, but this finale – like that of Beethoven's Eroica – brings the symphony to a vital culmination which is concerned, not so much with the expression of particular life-attitudes, as with the composer's artistic joy in symphonic creation, of building up a large musical structure. It thus follows naturally on the Adagietto, the haven of recuperation from life's turmoil; and this is further emphasized by the use of an actual *theme* from the Adagietto, at a quicker tempo, as the finale's second subject. Mahler's structure is a huge one, combining sonata and rondo, and including, as part of the opening group of themes, a fugal exposition on a bustling subject. The final climax, before the symphony races away to its cock-a-hoop conclusion, is a full restatement of the big brass chorale introduced so fleetingly towards the end of the second movement. Ultimately it is this explicit cross-reference between the most anguished movement in Part 1 and the most joyous movement of Part 111 which is the main cross-beam holding together the dangerously disparate elements of total darkness and total light at either end of the symphony.

Symphony No. 6 in A minor, *composed 1903–4; first performed at Essen, 1906, with Mahler conducting.*

In this awe-inspiring masterpiece Mahler, for the only time, embraced the normal symphonic conception – a four-movement orchestral work centred on one key: A minor sonata-allegro, E flat andante, A minor scherzo and rondo-finale. Despite its large time-scale (eighty minutes) and augmented orchestra (eight horns, six trumpets, four trombones), it is his most classical symphony. He provided no programme, even withdrawing his original title *The Tragic* – a name as general in its implications as 'Eroica' was to Beethoven.

*

There is something uniquely overwhelming about this particular symphony of Mahler, which may be due to its extremely personal inspiration. His wife, Alma, writing of the 'composing holidays' they spent with their two little daughters, said:

After he had drafted the first movement, he came down from the wood to tell me he had tried to express me in a theme. 'Whether I've succeeded, I don't know; but you'll have to put up with it.'
This is the great soaring theme of the first movement of the Sixth Symphony. In the third movement he represented the unrhythmical games of the two little children, tottering in zigzags over the sand. Ominously, the childish voices became more and more tragic, and at the end died out in a whimper. In the last movement he described himself and his downfall or, as he later said, his hero: 'It is the hero, on whom fall three blows of fate, the last of which fells him as a tree is felled'. Those were his words.
Not one of his works came as directly from his inmost heart as this. We both wept that day. The music and what it foretold touched us so deeply. . . .

Again, when Mahler first heard the music, while preparing the Essen première, he was quite overcome. The experience, moreover, was heightened by one of those curious coincidences that cropped up throughout his life:

None of his works moved him so deeply at its first hearing as this. We came to the last rehearsal, the dress-rehearsal – to the last movement with its three blows of fate. When it was over, Mahler walked up and down in the artists' room, sobbing, wringing his hands, unable to control himself. Fried, Gabrilovitch, Buths and I stood transfixed, not daring to look at one another. Suddenly Strauss came noisily in, noticing nothing. 'I say, Mahler, you've got to conduct some dead march or other tomorrow, before the Sixth – their mayor has died on them. So vulgar, that sort of thing – But what's the matter? What's up with you? But – ' and he went out as noisily as he had come in, quite unmoved, leaving us petrified. . . .*

Today we do not believe that composers 'foretell' their own fate in their music. Nevertheless, a year later, three blows did fall on Mahler, and the last one 'felled' him. In the spring his resignation was demanded at the Vienna

---

* In justice to Strauss, for whom Alma Mahler felt considerable antipathy, it should be noted that in fact Strauss himself conducted Mozart's *Masonic Funeral Music* at the beginning of the concert. [C.M.]

Opera; in July, his daughter Maria died, at the age of four; and a few days later, a doctor diagnosed Mahler's own fatal heart disease. Mahler was, of course, in Eliot's words already quoted, 'much possessed by death', and he was superstitious about it: he later went so far as to delete the 'prophetic' final hammer-blow in the symphony's finale.

All this explains why Mahler called the Sixth his 'Tragic' Symphony. It might seem strange for him to give this title to one particular work, when he is so widely regarded as altogether a 'tragic' composer. Yet after all, six of his eleven symphonic works – Nos. 1, 2, 3, 5, 7 and 8 – culminate in a blaze of triumph in the major; another – No. 4 – dies away in blissful serenity, also in the major; and three others – *The Song of the Earth*, No. 9 and No. 10 – fade out in resigned reconciliation, once more in the major. The Sixth alone offers no escape, ending starkly in the minor mode – that essential tragic symbol of the nineteenth-century composer.

The work was, in fact, the first genuine 'tragic symphony' to be written. The romantic concept of the heroic human struggle against fate, derived from Beethoven's Fifth, is its basis – but Beethoven's struggle has a triumphant outcome, as have those in several of Mahler's own symphonies. The purely tragic concept was first hinted at in Brahms's Fourth, which ends sternly in the minor; but the fierce vitality of the conclusion precludes any idea of a tragic catastrophe. Tchaikovsky's *Pathétique* certainly ends in utter darkness; but its mood of breast-beating despair is far removed from the objective universality of tragedy. In Mahler's Sixth, however, a truly tragic catastrophe, akin to those in Greek and Shakespearean drama, is presented with stark objectivity. And woven into it is a Hardy-like backcloth of nature, of mountain heights, far above human turmoil. This acts as a refuge in the slow movement, but in the first movement and finale as a purely elemental world, indifferent to human suffering.

The work's unique character has been briefly and powerfully summed up by Bruno Walter:

. . . the Sixth is bleakly pessimistic: it reeks of the bitter cup of human life. In contrast with the Fifth, it says 'No', above all in its last movement, where something resembling the inexorable strife of 'all against all' is translated into music. 'Existence is a burden; death is desirable and life hateful' might be its motto. . . . The mounting tension and climaxes of the last movement resemble, in their grim power, the mountainous waves of a sea that will overwhelm and destroy the ship; the work ends in hopelessness and the dark night of the soul. *Non placet* is his verdict on this world; the 'other world' is not glimpsed for a moment.

Walter views the symphony as a personal statement, and, as we have seen, its inspiration was extremely personal; moreover, the music, as always with Mahler, is as personal as music can be. How then can the work possess the objective universality of tragedy? Simply in that here, as nowhere else in Mahler's symphonies, his personal expression of dread and doom and disaster is subjected to an iron classical control, in two separate ways. First, although Mahler's formal command is always greater than is generally realized, only in the Sixth did he follow the traditional classical layout. Despite its characteristically vast time-scale and enormous orchestra, the symphony has neither vocal elements, nor direct quotations from songs, nor bird-calls, nor bugle-signals, nor passages in the popular style, nor any explicit programme. And not only does it consist of the traditional four movements, but three of them – the opening sonata movement with repeated exposition, the scherzo with trio, and the finale – are all in the same key of A minor.

But all this in itself could not have guaranteed classical control. The second, complementary means to this end was the objectifying of the thematic material itself, most of which (as so often with Bruckner) looks back beyond romantic lyricism to the motivic methods of the classical symphony: not to the actual classical *style* – the themes are too emotionally charged – but to the classical clarity and concision. These elements of course are partly present in Mahler's other symphonies; and there are still exceptions here, such as the opening movement's expansive lyrical second subject (the 'Alma' theme), the song-like main melody of the Andante moderato, and certain almost impressionistic passages in the finale's introduction. Nevertheless, the classical side of Mahler's complex musical personality is concentrated into this work far more potently than into any of his others; and this notwithstanding the length at which the material is developed, especially in the finale, which is practically a symphony in itself.

*

A tramping rhythm generates the first subject – a heroic-tragic march whose rock-like tonality is soon undermined by dissonance, until, after a bitter climax, it dies away with mutterings in the bass. Then follows the symphony's 'tragic' motto: a timpani march rhythm and (trumpets) a major triad fading to a minor one. After a quiet chorale passage (wind over pizzicato strings), the violins swing the music into F major, for the surging second subject, whose rather sentimental melodic idiom is vitalized by a passionate intensity. Reaching a tumultuous climax, it dies away tenderly. The development brings back the march more ominously, with grotesque woodwind trills and xylophone, but there is a sudden interruption – a vision, as of a mountain summit far above earthly strife: shimmering streams of chords on tremolando violins, with faint woodwind calls, through which the motto and the chorale theme echo on muted brass. Distant cowbells are heard – as Mahler once said, 'the last terrestrial sounds penetrating into the remote solitude of mountain peaks'. The music returns from the heights to resume the march of life, more confidently at first, but soon falling into the grim strains of the first subject for the recapitulation. This is more or less regular; the coda, beginning in darkness, rises to a triumphant A major statement of the 'Alma' theme.

The Andante* is a remote and lonely pastoral movement. The quiet opening theme initiates a little rocking figure on flutes, out of which a plaintive cor anglais melody appears. These three ideas are woven into pastoral moods of joy, yearning and deep heartache; the music passes through cloud and sunshine, at moments reaching the first movement's mountain peaks, but eventually ending in serene contentment.

The third movement returns to the battle of life with a vengeance, being the first of Mahler's 'horror' scherzos. A relentless, devilish, stamping dance begins, with pounding timpani, snarling trombones, and menacing woodwind trills with xylophone (from the first movement). Out of this emerges a fragile, innocent F major trio: timid, hesitant, childlike phrases, stumbling in changing time-signatures, like grave little toddlers at play (the marking is 'old-fashioned'). The scherzo alternates twice with this trio, dwarfing it, and often submerging it with the aid of the symphony's motto theme; at last 'the childish voices become more and more tragic, and at the end die out in a whimper'.

The voluminous finale presents 'the hero on whom fall three blows of fate, the last of which fells him as a tree is felled'; for these three climactic moments, Mahler took the unprecedented step of introducing a sledge-hammer into the score. The slow introduction presents the main material: a questing violin theme, soaring out of a dark impressionist texture only to be beaten down by the motto theme; a lugubrious phrase for solo tuba; a searching march tune for solo horn; a sombre brass chorale, which, on its second appearance, has a 'fate' motive in the bass, rising and falling in octaves, ninths and tenths. The main Allegro opens with a battling march, based on the tuba phrase; twice, over long periods, it wins through to a superhuman 'all-or-nothing' exultation; and twice the hammer-blow falls, the trombones blasting out the 'fate' theme, with trumpets blazing above it in stark two-part counterpoint. Once more the march sets off and rises to exultation; but this time it ends by going over into the opening music of the movement, for the questing violin theme to be beaten down by the motto as before. This is the moment for the third hammer-blow. The symphony ends with a doom-like coda – a slow, subdued, grindingly dissonant fugato on the 'fate' theme by trombones and tuba, and a final statement of the motto's timpani rhythm with only the minor triad above it, fading into silence.

---

* The symphony was first published with the scherzo placed second; but it was first performed with the Andante second, and subsequently republished twice during Mahler's lifetime with the movements in that order. Although the International Mahler Society edition of the work (1963) insists that the first published order should be re-adopted as the correct one, there is no clear evidence that Mahler wished to revert to it, and—on musical grounds as well as historical – the movements should undoubtedly be performed in the order described here. [c.m.]

SYMPHONY NO. 7, *composed 1904–5; first performed in Prague, 1908, under Mahler.*

For his last middle-period work, he still adhered to the purely orchestral symphony on a large scale (eighty minutes), though with a more or less normal orchestra. He brought back, however, the five-movement plan and progressive tonality of the Fifth – the same progression, minor to major, rising a semitone – returning to the affirmative mood of that work.

*

The Seventh is undoubtedly the Cinderella among Mahler's symphonies. It is probably the least well known, and of those who know it well, hardly anyone is prepared to praise it wholeheartedly – though there is general agreement as to the unique fascination of the three central movements. The truth is that No. 7, coming between two shattering masterpieces – the descent-into-hell of No. 6 and the heaven-storming No. 8 – presents an enigmatic, inscrutable face to the world: a most unusual attitude for a Mahler symphony and one which arouses suspicions as to its quality.

Yet one thing should make us pause before we class the Seventh as a partly fascinating but not fully achieved work of art. Schoenberg – by no means an out-and-out admirer of Mahler's music while Mahler was alive – was greatly impressed by the symphony. What he had to say, as we might expect, goes right to the heart of the matter, indicating the only possible way to approach the work, by pinpointing its anomalous position in Mahler's *œuvre*.

Schoenberg was already fully aware of the essentially biographical nature of Mahler's music. His letter to Mahler after hearing the Third Symphony in 1904 has already been quoted. What he said there is fundamental to Mahler's whole symphonic output – except only the Seventh; and Schoenberg promptly saw the difference. After he had heard the work in 1909, he wrote to Mahler:

'I had less than before the feeling of that sensational intensity which excites and lashes one on, which in a word moves the listener in such a way as to make him lose his balance without giving him anything in its place. On the contrary, I had the impression of perfect repose based on perfect harmony. . . . I have put you with the classical composers – but as one who to me is still a pioneer. I mean, there is surely a difference in being spared all extraneous excitement, in being at rest and in tranquillity, in the state in which beauty is enjoyed.'

Significantly, the 35-year-old Schoenberg (fourteen years younger than Mahler) was himself, at this time, moving away from the romantic conception of music as an outpouring of personal feeling, towards the modern classical (neo-classical) conception of 'absolute music'. In fact, already in 1906 he had begun exploiting the 'objective' procedure of superimposed fourths that plays such a prominent part in the first movement of Mahler's Seventh. No doubt he hit on this procedure quite independently, since he could not have known Mahler's unpublished score of 1905; nevertheless, as he admitted, the older composer was the pioneer. The fact is that such things were in the air (Satie had used fourths like this, in total obscurity, as early as 1891); and clearly, the hypersensitive Mahler, in the lull after the emotional exhaustion of composing the Sixth, found time to explore this potential new 'classical' development in the Seventh, before he plunged back, in the Eighth, into the subjective world of spiritual self-discovery which was his natural home. The Seventh is simply Mahler's 'neo-classical' symphony – pure music. There is no programme: the title which has been applied to it – 'The Song of the Night' – is merely someone's imaginative reaction to the conflict between sombre and glittering sonorities in the first movement, to the obviously nocturnal character of the central three movements, and the brilliant C major 'daylight' of the finale. This is a plausible interpretation, but in any case a purely poetic one. While it is inconceivable to think that there were no extra-musical influences at all behind the work – for instance, Mahler told his wife that the 'Serenade' (the fourth movement?) had been inspired by the murmuring streams and general German romanticism of the poetry of Eichendorff – he left himself free to exploit his musical imagination to the full, without any autobiographical intention. Consequently, the symphony is particularly fascinating in that it provides us with a direct view of his purely imaginative and technical interests in the new trends of modern music. For example, the first movement – slow introduction and Allegro alike – frequently reveals radical harmonic tendencies unsurpassed even in his later works, except for certain moments of great spiritual anguish in *The Song of the Earth*, the Ninth, and the unfinished Tenth. And, perhaps even more important, the whole work is a compendium of all that was most revolutionary in Mahler's orchestration: almost throughout the scoring is the most wildly fantastic ever conceived by this most wildly fantastic of orchestrators – a continual feast for the ear.

Even so, it is impossible not to feel that there remains something irreducibly problematic about this symphony. We should be wary of the current tendency to accept every extant statement of Schoenberg as 'the Gospel according to St Arnold'. In his letter to Mahler, Schoenberg continued: 'Which of the movements did I like best? Each of them!' Yet nearly all Mahler's admirers have settled for the central three – those superbly poetic stylizations of romantic genre-pieces, which draw continually on the style of the period's popular music in the most subtly creative way. The prowling nocturnal patrol of the first *Nachtmusik*, amidst echoing horn-calls and the indeterminate noises of night; the Hoffmannesque spookiness of the scherzo, with its opposition between 'things that go bump in the night' and puppet-like waltz music; the gurgling streams, the tinkling guitar and mandoline serenades of the second *Nachtmusik* – all these are haunting, uncanny music, opening magical windows on imagined worlds behind the visible world.

But there can be no question that the finale is largely a failure, and one feels that Schoenberg's indiscriminate praise was at least partly conditioned by his sense of the deference due to his more famous elder, which would naturally prevent him from expressing any reservations. It could be said that Mahler was not ideally cast as a classical composer, since only a deep spiritual or emotional compulsion could enable him to conceive material capable of filling his large canvases. Nevertheless, the first movement contains many magnificent things, some of them touching on the sublime (the chorale-phrases of the development section, for example). All in all, there is plenty and to spare of inspiration and imagination in the Seventh Symphony, which makes it far more worth hearing than many a symphony which is better-tailored because its creative scope is confined to a much narrower orbit.

✳

The large-scale first movement, an Adagio and Allegro con fuoco, carries further the tonal disruption of the Sixth: the superimposed fourths, bitonality, and violent key-switches from bar to bar, introduced new elements into the language of modern music. The Adagio introduction, in funeral march rhythm, foreshadows three ideas of the Allegro: a 'voice of nature' on tenor horn (reminiscent of the Third), a little modulating processional march for wind, and a stern trombone figure (deriving from the tenor horn theme). This last becomes the powerful march-like first subject of the E minor Allegro (a more thrusting version of the first theme in the Sixth). The second subject also recalls its counterpart in the Sixth, but its sentimentality is more languishing. Again as in the Sixth, the development concentrates on the march theme, grotesquely distorted, and has a visionary interlude – a wonderfully calm chorale-like passage with high string tremolando and mysterious fanfares. The recapitulation, introduced by an ennobled version of the introduction, is regular; the movement ends brilliantly with the march theme in E major.

The three central movements form a symmetrical group: two movements called 'Night Music' enclosing a scherzo no less nocturnal. The first 'Night Music', in C major-minor, is one of Mahler's most fantastic inspirations. Against an atmospheric background of horn calls answering one another over a distance, with 'nature-murmurs' and bird-calls ramifying on woodwind, a sauntering 'popular' tune (with sinister military march elements from 'Revelge') pursues its mysterious way like a wandering phantom. The presence of the motto theme of the Sixth half recalls the tragic mood of that work, as if in a disquieting dream.

The D minor scherzo is in the 'horror' vein of the one in the Sixth, but is less heavy. A whirling, ghostly dance on muted strings, pervaded with spasmodic rhythms on timpani and bass strings, alternates with a savagely distorted 'popular' waltz tune; the latter anticipates the scherzo of the Ninth, especially when sneered out viciously by fortissimo trombones. The movement, brilliantly imaginative as it is, lacks something of the personal impact

of its counterparts in the Sixth and Ninth; for once, Mahler seems to be standing outside the music.

The second 'Night Music', in F, is an intimate pastoral serenade, full of
liquid warblings of chalumeau clarinets and pluckings of harp, mandoline
and guitar. A singing horn tune alternates with themes of tenderness, longing and passion, the whole being kept within the stylized enchantment of the
serenade idiom. This is one of Mahler's most immediately attractive movements; it is surprising that it has never achieved the same kind of popularity
as the Adagietto of the Fifth Symphony.

The 'festive' C major finale opens with battering timpani, and wind and
horn fanfares. The main group comprises a major version of the first movement's march theme, on trumpet; a majestic progression of brass chords too
reminiscent of *The Mastersingers*; and a lively, jogging tune on wind and
strings which follows too relentlessly the pattern of one-note-up-and-two-
down. The subsidiary groups consist of 'popular' material of little distinction,
the second being of remarkable banality (unintentional for once). On its
second appearance, the jogging tune takes on an insistently chattering form
which is the most tiresome element of all. At the end, the first movement's
march theme returns in its original form, but in the major, to provide a
grandiose but unconvincing conclusion. Mahler had written for once the thing
he most detested – *Kapellmeistermusik*.

SYMPHONY NO. 8 IN E FLAT, *for three sopranos, two contraltos, tenor,
baritone, bass, double choir, boys' choir, orchestra and organ; composed 1906;
first performed at Munich, 1910, under Mahler – his one real triumph as a
composer in his lifetime.*

After the Seventh Symphony, Mahler was beset by fears of failing powers:
against the nihilism of the Sixth, left unanswered by the Seventh, what could
he oppose? One day, the words of the medieval Catholic hymn 'Veni Creator
Spiritus' came into his head; and, suddenly swept away on a great tide of
inspiration, he found himself composing the work which summed up his own
aspirations and those of post-revolutionary man. The setting of the hymn became a big symphonic first movement, enclosing a double fugue; later Mahler
set the final scene of Goethe's *Faust* as a complementary second part of the
symphony, synthesizing adagio, scherzo and finale.

*

After a performance of the Eighth Symphony in 1964, a reviewer expressed
surprise that the present writer, in the programme notes, should have said
that it 'is the Choral Symphony of the twentieth century, as Beethoven's

Ninth was the Choral Symphony of the nineteenth'. In his view, Stravinsky's
Symphony of Psalms has a far better claim to be regarded in this light; and
his view may seem to make sense – provided that one thinks only from the
point of view of musical style. The style of the Stravinsky is one of the radical
modern idioms of our century, whereas the Mahler, more than most of his
other works, draws heavily on the romantic idiom of the late nineteenth century. Even so, there are 'modernisms' in the Mahler; as early as bars 6 and 7
a diatonic canon produces two uncompromising clashes of a type which would
have shocked Wagner, but which was to become, two decades later, part and
parcel of Stravinsky's musical language during the neo-classical period of the
Symphony of Psalms.

However, the description of the Eighth as 'the Choral Symphony of the
twentieth century' was intended from the more general point of view of the
humanistic connotations of Beethoven's Ninth. In celebrating the brother-
hood of man in 1824, Beethoven's work voiced the aspirations of the first,
optimistic period of humanism; and Mahler's Eighth Symphony, written at a
time (1906) when the optimism of the first period had completely foundered,
stands as a determined restatement of mankind's aspirations for the second
humanistic period – our own – which is riddled with doubt and despair. Seen
from this wider cultural point of view, Stravinsky's *Symphony of Psalms* has
no special significance: it is the product of a personal adherence to a particular
'timeless' religious dogma in an age which has largely abandoned religion in
favour of humanism, and it anyway makes no attempt to inspire the listener
with any 'message', but has the more modest aim of impressing him with its
purely artistic excellence as a piece of music. And from this point of view,
too, the question of idiom is irrelevant: the eventual replacing of Beethoven's
idiom by that of Wagner does not prevent his Ninth from remaining an all-
important human document of the nineteenth century; nor does the super-
session of Mahler's idiom by those of Stravinsky and others prevent his
Eighth from remaining an all-important human document of our own century.

Curiously enough, the Latin text that Mahler chose for the first of the
symphony's two parts inhabits the same 'timeless' religious world as the Latin
texts of Stravinsky's *Symphony of Psalms*. 'Veni Creator Spiritus' is the Office
Hymn for Second Vespers of Pentecost, but Mahler's treatment of it is quite
different from any liturgical treatment: the poem, which is the orthodox
Christian's humble prayer for the enlightenment of Pentecost, becomes, in
Mahler's thunderous military-march setting, a great confident shout by humanity to the skies for the creative vision that the modern world so desperately
needs. Not that doubt and despair are not also present in the music – in the
plea to 'fortify our weak frames with your eternal strength' and the devilish
orchestral distortions of the 'confident' themes which link the two appearances of this plea; but doubt and despair are dispelled once and for all by
the incandescent outburst at the words 'Illuminate our senses, pour love into
our hearts!'

If this religious text of Part I is given a secular, humanistic meaning, the humanistic text of the symphony's second part – the closing scene of Goethe's *Faust* – is given a timeless, metaphysical meaning at the work's culmination, where the famous last eight lines of Goethe's great dramatic poem are set as a religious chorale. Faust, the searcher for secret, forbidden knowledge – prototype of, amongst other things, the scientists who have made the dangerous discoveries of the hydrogen bomb and the industrial processes which are polluting the earth's atmosphere – had been condemned to Hell by every writer who dramatized his story; but the humanistic Goethe imagined him escaping from the devil's clutches and finding redemption. Faust is, after all, Goethe seems to say, a symbol of questing humanity, and the various aspects of humanity's quest cannot be separated from one another: if it leads at times to widespread folly and wholesale catastrophe, it still survives and continues, impelled by a desire to struggle onwards and upwards. And the belief of Goethe and Mahler – certainly hard to cling to in times such as ours – is that the quest will eventually succeed, by culminating in the metaphysical experience of absolute wisdom, power and love. It is in this sense that Mahler's Eighth is the Choral Symphony of the twentieth century: like Beethoven's, but in a different way, it sets before us an ideal which we are as yet far from realizing – even perhaps moving away from – but which we can hardly abandon without perishing.

*

The Eighth Symphony belongs to neither the middle nor last periods, but stands on its own. Apart from much clashing counterpoint in Part I, and certain tonal disruptions in Part II, Mahler temporarily abandoned the more progessive elements of his style; instead he united his masterly middle-period orchestral polyphony with the firm tonality, monumental apparatus and all-embracing programmatic aim of the Second Symphony, setting a seal on all his achievements hitherto. The sheer size of the work might suggest megalomania, but Mahler needed it to express his tremendous concept. The huge forces (responsible for the non-Mahler title 'Symphony of a Thousand'), as well as the large-scale forms, are handled with extraordinary clarity. What flaws there may be are part and parcel of a work which strives so heroically to elevate man to the stature of a god.

The symphony remains firmly centred on E flat throughout. Part I bursts out with a mighty choral invocation – the basic theme of the work – immediately transformed by trombones into a march theme which will be used pervasively to unify the movement. The first group culminates in a long soaring theme, *fortissimo*, beginning on unison male voices. The soloists dominate the supplicatory second group (D flat and A flat), begun quietly by the soprano; the end of the exposition comes with thoughts of human frailty – a shadowy D minor version of the opening invocation. The development begins orchestrally with 'the spirit that denies', grotesquely distorting the confident march music, evoking further supplications from the soloists. Then the music tenses up for the unforgettable moment: the cry for illumination and love – a new theme – hurled out in E major by soloists and chorus in unison, backed by the full orchestra and organ. The boys' choir enters with another new theme – a carol-like song of joy. After a big climax, a fierce battle march begins in E minor ('Scatter the foe'), leading to the apex of the movement – the double fugue ('Our leader, go before'); this is a long triumphal march (in E flat) based on the original march tune and the 'soaring' theme. A balancing restatement of the 'illumination' theme, in E again, leads back to the E flat recapitulation. This is much condensed, omitting the 'shadowy' material; a jubilant coda, opening in D flat with the boys singing the Gloria, reviews all the main themes; and an extra brass choir crowns the whole movement with jubilant statements of the 'illumination' and 'soaring' themes.

Part 1 is tautly symphonic, befitting its lapidary Latin text; Part 11, developing the same materials in late romantic style, mirrors Goethe's more rhapsodic language. The first section, the Adagio in E flat minor, opens on earth, with mystic utterances of anchorites in a craggy wooded wilderness. It begins with an orchestral exposition: bare 'forest' music (pizzicato bass-motive, flute and clarinet theme); yearning music (a passionate horn melody); dark, wild, 'nature' music (violently leaping string figures); and a joyful little march on flutes, looking towards the scherzo section. The whole is then recapitulated in varied form, with voices: whispering male chorus; Pater Ecstaticus (baritone), turning the horn theme warmly to the major; Pater Profundus (bass), developing the 'nature' music into the 'illumination' theme, referring to 'messengers of love'.

The scherzo section (in various keys) leaves the earth, as angels (women's and boys' voices) bear Faust's soul upwards. The music uses the 'illumination' theme, the carol-like tune, and a new 'innocent' grazioso melody. Memories of mortality bring back the shadowy music of Part 1; after which the flutes' little march tune reappears. From on high, Doctor Marianus (tenor) sings a long impassioned eulogy of Mater Gloriosa (Mary), bridging over to the finale.

This opens softly in E with a floating theme on violins, the chorus accompanying with hushed harmonies. A solo soprano (a Penitent) joins the chorus; then, one by one, three other female voices (also Penitents) sing extended solo supplications, followed by a trio in canon. Soon Gretchen's voice is heard, singing the floating violin theme, which continues on the orchestra with a lively counter-theme by the boys' voices. Gretchen's voice returns, describing Faust's transfiguration (which brings references to the opening of Part 1); and the voice of Mater Gloriosa calls Faust to higher spheres. Then follows the final peroration, which draws together all the threads with symphonic mastery. Begun by Doctor Marianus, it is taken up by the choir, and leads through an orchestral transformation to the final chorale – the 'Chorus Mysticus' (derived from the music of Pater Ecstaticus). Beginning in a whisper, it swells quietly (the soprano soloists soaring with the 'illumination' theme) to a fortissimo climax. There is a majestic orchestral coda; at the end the separate brass blaze out the symphony's opening theme, followed by the original trombone march theme in a new version which reaches imperiously to the heights.

Part ɪ
HYMN: VENI, CREATOR SPIRITUS

First Group

Veni, creator spiritus,
Mentes tuorum visita;

Come, Creator Spirit,
Dwell in our minds;

Second Group

Imple superna gratia
Quae tu creasti pectora.

Fill with divine grace
The hearts of thy servants.

Qui Paraclitus diceris,
Donum Dei altissimi,

Thou named the Comforter,
Gift of God most high,

Fons vivus, ignis, caritas,
Et spiritualis unctio.

Source of life, fire, love,
And soul's anointing.

Codetta

Infirma nostri corporis
Virtute firmans perpeti.

Our weak frames
Fortify with thine eternal strength.

Soloists

Infirma nostri corporis
Virtute firmans perpeti.

Our weak frames
Fortify with thine eternal strength.

New theme

Accende lumen sensibus,
Infunde amorem cordibus!

Illuminate our senses,
Pour love into our hearts!

March

Hostem repellas longius,
Pacemque dones protinus.

Scatter the foe,
Grant us thy peace.

Double Fugue

Ductore sic te praevio,
Vitemus omne pessimum;
Tu septiformis munere,
Dextrae paternae digitus.

Our leader, go before,
That we may shun all evil;
Grant us thy sevenfold blessing,
Thou right hand of the Father,

Per te sciamus da patrem,
Noscamus atque filium,
Te utriusque spiritum
Credamus omni tempore.

Grant us knowledge of the Father,
And of the Son,
And of thee, O Spirit,
Now and evermore.

Restatement of new theme

Accende lumen sensibus,
Infunde amorem cordibus!

Illuminate our senses,
Pour love into our hearts!

First Group

Veni, Creator Spiritus,

Come, Creator Spirit,

Second Group

Qui Paraclitus diceris,
Donum Dei altissimi,
Da gratiorum munera,
Da gaudiorum praemia,
Dissolve litis vincula,
Adstringe pacis foedera,
Ductore sic te praevio,
Vitemus omne pessimum.

Thou named the Comforter,
Gift of God most high,
Grant us thy saving grace,
Grant the foretaste of bliss,
Free us from bonds of strife,
Bind us with pacts of peace.
Our leader, go before,
That we may shun all evil.

Coda
Orchestra, leading to

Gloria Patri Domino,
Natoque, qui a mortuis
Surrexit, ac Paraclito
In saeculorum saecula.

Glory be to God the Father,
And to the Son, who from the dead
Arose, and to the Paraclete,
From everlasting to everlasting.

Part II
FINAL SCENE FROM FAUST

CHORUS OF ANCHORITES AND ECHO

Waldung, sie schwankt heran,
Felsen, sie lasten dran,
Wurzeln, sie klammern an,
Stamm dicht an Stamm hinan.
Woge nach Woge spritzt,
Höhle, die tiefste, schützt.
Löwen, sie schleichen stumm-
Freundlich um uns herum,
Ehren geweihten Ort,
Heiligen Liebeshort.

Woods clamber tremblingly,
Crags bear down weightily,
Roots cling tenaciously,
Trunks make a density;
Spurting of wave on wave –
Deep lies our hermits' cave.
Lions around in dumb
Friendliness gently come,
Honour our sanctuary,
Love's holy privacy.

PATER ECSTATICUS *(hovering up and down)*

Ewiger Wonnebrand,	*Rapture which yearns ever,*
Glühendes Liebeband,	*Love-bond which burns ever,*
Siedender Schmerz der Brust,	*Pain in me seething up,*
Schäumende Gotteslust.	*Love of God foaming up.*
Pfeile, durchdringet mich,	*Arrows, pierce through me and,*
Lanzen, bezwinget mich,	*Lances, subdue me and,*
Keulen, zerschmettert mich,	*Clubs, leave no form in me,*
Blitze, durchwettert mich!	*Thunderstorms, storm in me!*
Dass ja das Nichtige	*That now the Nothingness*
Alles verflüchtige,	*Drown all in emptiness,*
Glänze der Dauerstern,	*One constant star must shine,*
Ewiger Liebe Kern.	*Kernel of love divine.*

PATER PROFUNDUS *(from the depths)*

Wie Felsenabgrund mir zu Füssen	*As at my feet a craggy chasm*
Auf tiefem Abgrund lastend ruht,	*Weighs on a deeper chasm's prop,*
Wie tausend Bäche strahlend fliessen	*As streams in thousands flow and sparkle*
Zum grausen Sturz des Schaums der Flut,	*Towards the dread rapids' foaming drop,*
Wie stark mit eignem kräftigen Triebe	*As with its own strong urge the tree-trunk*
Der Stamm sich in die Lüfte trägt:	*Climbs up the air, erect and tall,*
So ist es die allmächtige Liebe,	*Even so is that almighty love*
Die alles bildet, alles hegt.	*Which all things forms and fosters all.*
Ist um mich her ein wildes Brausen,	*Around me here a frantic rushing*
Als wogte Wald und Felsengrund,	*Makes wood and cleft a stormy sea,*
Und doch stürzt, liebevoll im Sausen,	*Yet full of love the water's fullness*
Die Wasserfülle sich zum Schlund,	*Roars as it plumbs the cavity,*
Berufen gleich, das Tal zu wässern;	*Ordained to straightway feed the valley;*
Der Blitz, der flammend niederschlug,	*The thunderbolt which crashed in flame*
Die Atmosphäre zu verbessern,	*To cleanse the air which bore within it*
Die Gift und Dunst im Busen trug,	*Poison and evil mists, these same*
Sind Liebesboten, sie verkünden,	*Are messengers of love, announcing*
Was ewig schaffend uns umwallt.	*What round us ever moves and makes.*
Mein Inn'res mög' es auch entzünden,	*May that light kindle too within me*
Wo sich der Geist, verworren, kalt,	*Where the cold spirit gropes and quakes,*
Verquält in stumpfer Sinne Schranken,	*Self-racked in body's bonds of dullness,*
Scharfangeschloss'nem Kettenschmerz.	*Riveted fast in chains that smart.*
O Gott! beschwichtige die Gedanken,	*O God, have mercy on my thoughts,*
Erleuchte mein bedürftig Herz!	*Give light to my impoverished heart!*

ANGELS *(floating in the higher air, carrying the immortal part of Faust)*

Gerettet ist des edle Glied	*Saved, saved now is that precious part*
Der Geisterwelt vom Bösen:	*Of our spirit world from evil:*
"Wer immer strebend sich bemüht,	*'Should a man strive with all his heart,*

E

Den können wir erlösen."
Und hat an ihm die Liebe gar
Von oben teilgenommen,
Begegnet ihm die selige Schar
Mit herzlichem Willkommen.

Heaven can foil the devil.'
And if love also from on high
Has helped him through his sorrow,
The hallowed legions of the sky
Will give him glad good morrow.

BLESSED BOYS *(circling round the highest peak)*

Hände verschlinget
Freudig zum Ringverein,
Regt euch und singet
Heil'ge Gefühle drein!
Göttlich belehret,
Dürft ihr vertrauen;
Den ihr verehret,
Werdet ihr schauen.

Joyfully gyring
Dance ye in union,
Hands linked and choiring
Blessed communion!
Pattern before you,
Godly, to cheer you,
Whom you adore, you
Soon shall see near you.

THE YOUNGER ANGELS

Jene Rosen, aus den Händen
Liebend-heiliger Büsserinnen
Halfen uns den Sieg gewinnen,
Und das hohe Werk vollenden,
Diesen Seelenschatz erbeuten.
Böse wichen, als wir streuten,
Teufel flohen, als wir trafen.
Statt gewohnter Höllenstrafen
Fühlten Liebesqual die Geister;
Selbst der alte Satansmeister
War von spitzer Pein durchdrungen.
Jauchzet auf! es is gelungen.

Ah those roses, their donation –
Lovely-holy penitent women –
Helped us to defend Apollyon,
Brought our work to consummation,
To this priceless spirit's capture.
Devils, as we scattered rapture,
Struck by roses, fled in panic,
Feeling not their pains Satanic
But the pains of love's disaster;
Even that old Satan-master
Felt a torment arrowed, marrowed,
Alleluia! Hell is harrowed.

THE MORE PERFECT ANGELS

Uns bleibt ein Erdenrest
Zu tragen peinlich,
Und wär' er von Asbest,
Er ist nicht reinlich.
Wenn starke Geisteskraft
Die Elemente
An sich herangerafft,
Kein Engel trennte
Geeinte Zwienatur
Der innigen beiden,
Die ewige Liebe nur
Vermag's zu scheiden.

This scrap of earth, alas,
We must convoy it;
Were it asbestos, yet
Earth would allow it.
When soul's dynamic force
Has drawn up matter
Into itself, then no
Angel could shatter
The bonds of that twoness –
The oneness that tied it;
Eternal love alone
Knows to divide it.

THE YOUNGER ANGELS

Ich spür soeben,
Nebelnd um Felsenhöh,
Ein Geisterleben
Regend sich in der Näh'.

Close, round the mountain top,
To my perceiving
Moves like a mist a
Spiritual living.

Seliger Knaben	*I see a sainted flight:*
Seh' ich bewegte Schaar,	*Children unmeshed from*
Los von der Erde Druck	*Meshes of earth, they*
Im Kreis gesellt,	*Fly in a ring,*
Die sich erlaben	*Being refreshed from*
Am neuen Lenz und Schmuck	*Heaven's rebirth they*
Der obern Welt.	*Bask in its spring.*
Sei er zum Anbeginn	*Faust, to begin to rise*
Steigendem Vollgewinn	*Towards highest Paradise,*
Diesen gesellt.	*With them must wing.*
(Lines transposed; one omitted)	*(One line omitted)*

DOCTOR MARIANUS *(in the highest, purest cell)*

Hier ist die Aussicht frei,	*Here is the prospect free,*
Der Geist erhoben.	*Spirit-uplifting.*
Dort ziehen Frauen vorbei,	*Yonder to women's shapes*
Schwebend nach oben.	*Over me drifting;*
Die Herrliche mittenin	*And, wreathed in her seven*
Im Sternenkranze,	*Bright stars, they attend her –*
Die Himmelskönigin,	*The high Queen of Heaven;*
Ich seh's am Glanze.	*I gaze on her splendour.*

BLESSED BOYS

Freudig empfangen wir	*Gladly receiving this*
Diesen im Puppenstand;	*Chrysalid entity,*
Also erlangen wir	*Now we achieve, in this,*
Englisches Unterpfand.	*Angels' identity.*
Löset die Flocken los,	*Let the cocoon which is*
Die ihn umgeben!	*Round him be broken!*
Schon ist er schön und gross	*Great! Fair! How soon he is*
Von heiligem Leben.	*Heaven-awoken!*

DOCTOR MARIANUS *(enraptured)*

Höchste Herrscherin der Welt!	*Highest empress of the world,*
Lasse mich im blauen,	*Let these blue and sacred*
Ausgespannten Himmelszelt	*Tents of heaven here unfurled*
Dein Geheimnis schauen.	*Show me now thy secret!*
Bill'ge, was des Mannes Brust	*Sanction that which in man's breast*
Ernst und zart bewegt	*Soft and strong prepares him –*
Und mit heil'ger Liebeslust	*Love which joyful, love which blest*
Dir entgegen trägt.	*Towards thy presence bears him.*
Unbezwinglich unser Mut,	*Thine august commands are such,*
Wenn du hehr gebietest;	*Nothing can subdue us –*
Plötzlich milderst sich die Glut,	*Fires burn gentler at thy touch*
Wenn du uns befriedest.	*Should thy peace imbue us.*
Jungfrau, rein im schönsten Sinne,	*Virgin, pure as none are pure,*
Mutter, Ehren würdig,	*Mother, pearl of honour,*
Uns erwählte Königin,	*Chosen as our queen, the sure*
Göttern ebenbürtig.	*Godhead stamped upon her!*

99

CHORUS

Dir, der Unberührbaren,
Ist es nicht benommen,
Dass die leicht Verführbaren
Traulich zu dir kommen.
In die Schwachheit hingerafft
Sind sie schwer zu retten;
Wer zerreisst aus eig'ner Kraft
Der Gelüste Ketten?
Wie entgleitet schnell der Fuss
Schiefem, glattem Boden?

Thou, albeit immaculate,
It is of thy fashion
That the easily seduced
Sue to thy compassion.
Such whom frailty reft, are hard,
Hard to save, if ever;
Who can burst the bonds of lust
Through his own endeavour?
Do not sliding gradients cause
Sudden slips?

CHORUS OF PENITENTS

Du schwebst zu Höhen
Der ewigen Reiche,
Vernimm das Flehen,
Du Ohnegleiche!
Du Gnadenreiche!

Mary, in soaring
To kingdoms eternal,
Hear our imploring
Thou beyond rival!
Fount of survival!

MAGNA PECCATRIX

Bei der Liebe, die den Füssen
Deines gottverklärten Sohnes
Tränen liess zum Balsam fliessen,
Trotz des Pharisäerhohnes;
Beim Gefässe, das so reichlich
Tropfte Wohlgeruch hernieder,
Bei den Locken, die so weichlich
Trockneten die heil'gen Glieder –

By my love which mingled tears with
Balm to bathe His feet, revering
Him thy Son, now God-transfigured,
When the Pharisees were jeering;
By that vessel which so sweetly
Split its perfumed wealth profusely,
By my hair which dried those holy
Limbs, around them falling loosely –

MULIER SAMARITANA

Bei dem Bronn, zu dem schon weiland
Abram liess die Herde führen,
Bei dem Eimer, der dem Heiland
Kühl die Lippe durft' berühren;
Bei der reinen, reichen Quelle,
Die nun dorther sich ergiesset,
Überflüssig, ewig helle
Rings durch alle Welten fliesst –

By the well where Father Abram
Watered once his flocks when marching,
By the bucket once allowed to
Touch and cool Christ's lips when parching;
By that pure and generous source which
Now extends its irrigation,
Overbrimming, ever-crystal,
Flowering through the whole creation –

MARIA AEGYPTIACA

Bei dem hochgeweihten Orte,
Wo den Herrn man niederliess,
Bei dem Arm, der von der Pforte
Warnend mich zurücke stiess;
Bei der vierzigjährigen Busse,
Der ich treu in Wüsten blieb,
Bei dem seligen Scheidegrusse,
Den im Sand ich niederschrieb –

By that more than sacred garden
Where they laid the Lord to rest,
By the arm which from the portal
Thrust me back with stern behest;
By my forty years' repentance
Served out in a desert land,
By the blessed word of parting
Which I copied in the sand –

THE THREE

Die du grossen Sünderinnen	*Thou who to most sinning women*
Deine Nähe nicht verweigerst	*Thy dear presence ne'er deniest,*
Und ein büssendes Gewinnen	*Raising us repentant women*
In die Ewigkeiten steigerst,	*To eternities the highest,*
Gönn auch dieser guten Seele,	*Make to this good soul concession –*
Die sich einmal nur vergessen,	*Only once misled by pleasure*
Die nicht ahnte, dass sie fehle,	*To a never-dreamt transgression;*
Dein Verzeihen angemessen!	*Grant her pardon in her measure.*

A PENITENT *(once named Gretchen)*

Neige, neige,	*Uniquely tender,*
Du Ohnegleiche,	*Thou queen of splendour,*
Du Strahlenreiche,	*Thy visage render*
Dein Antlitz gnädig meinem Glück!	*Benign towards my felicity!*
Der früh Geliebte,	*My love of old, he*
Nicht mehr Getrübte,	*Is now consoled, he*
Er kommt zurück.	*Comes back to me.*

BLESSED BOYS *(approaching, flying in circles)*

Er überwächst uns schon	*Passing beyond us*
An mächtigen Gliedern,	*So soon in resplendence,*
Wird treuer Pflege Lohn	*He will make ample*
Reichlich erwidern	*Return for our tendance;*
Wir wurden früh entfernt	*Early we left the*
Von Lebechören;	*Terrestrial chorus;*
Doch dieser hat gelernt,	*He will instruct us,*
Er wird uns lehren.	*Instructed before us.*

THE SINGLE PENITENT *(once named Gretchen)*

Vom edlen Geisterchor umgeben,	*By choirs of noble souls surrounded*
Wird sich der Neue kaum gewahr,	*This new one scarcely feels his soul,*
Er ahnet kaum das frische Leben,	*Can scarcely sense this life unbounded,*
So gleicht er schon der heiligen Schar.	*Yet fills at once his heavenly role.*
Sieh! wie er jedem Erdenbande	*See how he sheds the earthly leaven,*
Der alten Hülle sich entrafft	*Tears off each shroud of old untruth,*
Und aus ätherischem Gewande	*And from apparel woven in heaven,*
Hervortritt erste Jugendkraft!	*Shines forth his pristine power of youth!*
Vergönne mir, ihn zu belehren,	*Mary, grant me to instruct him,*
Noch blendet ihn der neue Tag.	*Dazzled as yet by this new day.*

MATER GLORIOSA

Komm! hebe dich zu höhern Sphären!	*Come then! To higher spheres conduct him!*
Wenn er dich ahnet, folgt er nach.	*Divining you, he knows the way.*

101

D O C T O R   M A R I A N U S *(bowing in adoration)*

Blicket auf zum Retterblick,
Alle reuig Zarten,
Euch zu sel'gem Glück,
Dankend umzuarten!
Werde jeder bess're Sinn
Dir zum Dienst erbötig;
Jungfrau, Mutter, Königin,
Göttin, bleibe gnädig!

All your tender penitents,
Gaze on her who saves you —
Thus you change your lineaments
And salvation laves you.
To her feet each virtue crawl,
Let her will transcend us;
Virgin, Mother, Queen of All,
Goddess, still befriend us!

C H O R U S   M Y S T I C U S

Alles Vergängliche
Ist nur ein Gleichnis;
Das Unzulängliche,
Hier wird's Ereignis;
Das Unbeschreibliche,
Hier ist's getan;
Das Ewig-Weibliche
Zieht uns hinan.

All that is past of us
Was but reflected;
All that was lost in us
Here is corrected;
All indescribables
Here we descry;
Eternal Womanhead
Leads us on high.

(*From Goethe's* Faust *translated by Louis MacNeice, published by Faber and Faber.*)

The Eighth Symphony was Mahler's last affirmation; in 1907 the 'three blows of fate' descended on him, and the last 'felled him as a tree is felled'. Waking from his vision of mankind redeemed to find himself in the valley of the shadow of death before his time, what could he now set against 'the spirit that denies'? The vision remained valid – for humanity; but it was no comfort for the individual faced with disintegration. The affirmation of vitality of the First and Fifth Symphonies was impossible; the faith of the Second, Third and Fourth ungraspable; and the nihilism of the Sixth unthinkable. Spiritual defeat stared Mahler in the face. He was forced back on his one indestructible possession – his intense love of living. In his last period, he refused to allow his belief in the beauty and joy of life to be destroyed by his physically depressing illness, his own tormented and tormenting spirit, or even by the grinning horror of death itself. He wrung from defeat an ultimate vindication of human existence. The last works are undeniably a heart-broken farewell to life, but a loving, not a bitter one. A pessimistic attitude? It is given to very few to 'take fate by the throat' like Beethoven – or to face fate as boldly and go down fighting as courageously as Mahler.

DAS LIED VON DER ERDE (THE SONG OF THE EARTH), *for tenor, contralto (or baritone), and orchestra, composed 1907–8; first performed after Mahler's death, in Munich, 1911, under Bruno Walter.*

Mahler called the work a symphony, and in the Mahlerian sense, *The Song of the Earth* – a setting of six old Chinese poems in translations by Hans Bethge – is a symphony: first movement, conflict; four shorter movements bearing on the central idea; complex finale bringing a resolution; the whole composed of motives developed symphonically, if not in traditional forms. Mahler only refused to call it 'No. 9' out of superstitious dread: Beethoven and Bruckner had got no further than nine, and he half seriously hoped to cheat death yet by stopping his numbering at eight.

The last, appalling tension in Mahler's spirit forced from him music of indescribable beauty and poignancy. The clarity of the instrumentation (for normal orchestra with extra wind) is as masterly as ever, but the hardness has practically vanished; in the main, the lines are sharper and thinner, or fainter and more disembodied. The material, evoking a quasi-Chinese atmosphere with the pentatonic scale, and often advancing further the tonal disruption of the Sixth and Seventh Symphonies, is full of deep heartache; this is Mahler's most purely personal style. The use of tonality is largely psychological, yet a 'progression' can be discerned – inevitably a falling one: the tonal sequence of the first five movements (A minor, D minor, B flat, G, A) implies a finale in D (minor), but in fact it is a tone lower, in C minor.

*

'No young man believes he shall ever die.' This statement opens Hazlitt's essay 'On the Feeling of Immortality in Youth', and it is true – even of those sensitive individuals who are haunted by death-longings during adolescence and early manhood. The young acknowledge human mortality as an inescapable fact, and some of them dwell on it, but they do not apprehend its existential significance in relation to themselves; they are too much alive.

With Mahler, these early death-longings took the familiar romantic form of a mystical sense of oneness with nature, in consoling contrast to his feeling of being isolated in an unsympathetic human society: they figure as a desire to be absorbed back, out of the repugnant flux of human life, into the peace of the infinite. In 1879, when he was nineteen, he wrote in a letter to his intimate friend, Josef Steiner:

> Oh my beloved earth, when, oh when, will you take the forsaken one to your breast? Behold, mankind has banished him from itself, and he flees from its cold and heartless bosom to you, to you! Oh care for the lonely one, the restless one, Universal Mother!

The phraseology is stilted, and suggests the theatrical attitudinizing characteristic of the romantic youth of the nineteenth century; yet with Mahler the sentiments were genuine enough. He had been closely acquainted with premature death amongst his several brothers and sisters, and with early insanity amongst his friends and acquaintances; and the balance of his sensitive nature had been disturbed in a way which was to drive one of his surviving brothers to madness and the other to suicide. Indeed, his preoccupation with the thought of death was to remain with him throughout his life: practically all his works sprang from it, in one way or another. And in *The Song of the*

Earth, completed less than three years before his own death, we find a more profound fusion of the ideas of death and nature which he had expressed so callowly thirty years earlier in his youthful letter to Steiner.

When, in 1907, a friend sent him a recently-published volume of poetry called 'The Chinese Flute' – translations from the Chinese by Hans Bethge – the poem he chose to set as the opening movement of *The Song of the Earth* was one by Li-Tai-Po containing the lines:

> Das Firmament blaut ewig, und die Erde
> Wird lange fest steh'n und aufblüh'n im Lenz.
> Du aber, Mensch, wie lang lebst denn du?

> *(The firmament is blue eternally, and the earth*
> *Will long stand fast and blossom in spring.*
> *But you, O man, for how long do you live?)*

Furthermore, for the ending of the whole work, Mahler set some lines added by himself, which recall this passage in the first movement and at the same time echo his love of the earth which he had expressed in his letter to Steiner:

> Die liebe Erde allüberall
> Blüht auf im Lenz und grünt aufs neu!
> Allüberall und ewig blauen licht die Fernen!
> Ewig . . . Ewig. . . .

> *(The dear earth everywhere*
> *Blossoms in spring and grows green again!*
> *Everywhere and forever the distance shines*
> *   bright and blue!*
> *Forever ... forever....)*

'The dear earth' . . . 'Oh my beloved earth' . . . and yet there is a great difference. In 1879, the earth had seemed a Universal Mother that would receive back and comfort her forsaken child, who would continue in some mystical way to exist as part of her; but in 1907, the earth, though still beloved, is now simply itself, a separate entity that will continue blossoming and growing green again for ever, as opposed to the individual human being, who once extinct will no longer be there to know of it. Although at the age of nineteen, and for nearly thirty years afterwards, the thought of death had remained persistently in Mahler's mind, it had been conceived in living images: as a haven of peace (in the letter to Steiner and in the song-cycles *Lieder eines fahrenden Gesellen* and *Kindertotenlieder*); as a hideous nightmare to be shaken off by furious vital activity (in the First, Fifth and Seventh Symphonies); or as the gateway into the 'eternal life' of the Christian faith (in the Second, Third, Fourth and Eighth). Only in the Sixth does the inescapable Mahlerian funeral march triumph in the end; and here there is an objective universality, akin to Greek tragedy, which elevates the music above considerations of the fate of the individual. 'No young man believes he shall ever die'. But when Mahler came to compose *The Song of the Earth*, he found himself face to face with death as an existential reality – as the imminent cessation of his own life.

Once his doctor had pronounced him a doomed man, death ceased to be any kind of image, but appeared as its naked self, and Mahler's longing was now entirely for life: 'I am thirstier than ever for life' he wrote to Bruno Walter in 1908. And it is this sense of existential reality which explains the uniquely harrowing character of the music of *The Song of the Earth* in Mahler's *œuvre* up to that time. If his earlier works had been full of *images* of mortality, this one is permeated with the bitter *taste* of mortality. It is indeed the song of the *earth* – of the world of transience and dissolution – as opposed to the preceding Eighth Symphony's 'song of *heaven*' – of the world of eternity and immortality. Mahler's hard-won religious faith had deserted him, and left him with only the certain facts of earthly life and death.

A letter of 1909 to Bruno Walter reveals his bewildered state of mind:

> If I am to find my way back to myself, I have got to accept the horrors of loneliness. I speak in riddles, since you do not know what has gone on and is going on within me. It is, assuredly, no hypochondriac fear of death, as you suppose. I have long known that I have got to die. . . .

Yes, but 'no young man *believes* he shall ever die'. The letter continues:

> Without trying to explain or describe something for which there probably are no words, I simply say that at a single fell stroke I have lost any calm and peace of mind I ever achieved. I stand *vis-à-vis de rien* [face to face with nothing], and now, at the end of my life, I have to begin to learn to walk and stand.

This letter sets the scene for Mahler's last-period trilogy – *The Song of the Earth*, the Ninth Symphony, and the uncompleted Tenth. These three works represent a three-stage pilgrimage in the process of 'learning to walk and stand' – learning to find a meaning in life on the threshold of death without the assurance of any religious faith in immortality. In *The Song of the Earth*, the first stage, the sudden bitter awareness of imminent extinction is confronted and fused with a hedonistic delight in the beauty of nature and the ecstasy of living, both now possessed so briefly and precariously. Then, in the second stage, the Ninth Symphony, this evidently goalless hedonism becomes a mere starting-point which vanishes as bitterness and horror come uppermost with terrible violence and lead to ultimate heartbreak. Finally, in the third stage, the Tenth Symphony, a deeper self-exploration eventually exorcises bitterness, horror and heartbreak, and culminates in a hymn to human love and a serene, unlamenting acceptance of the inevitable human lot.

This means that *The Song of the Earth* still remains unique, even in comparison with the two works which followed it. The first stage of Mahler's process of 'learning' was a poignant dual awareness of the bitterness of mortality and the sweet sensuous ecstasy of being alive, mixed in equal measure – an almost unbearable union of opposites which resulted in a strangely insubstantial and disembodied poetic vision. It is as if the sudden taste of mortality had dissolved all solidity out of the world, leaving it sharply etched in thin lines and clear water-colours. These are, of course, appropriate to the Chinese atmosphere of the text, and in fact this particular text reached Mahler from his friend at a miraculously appropriate moment in his life. *The Song of the Earth* has a new, naked kind of harmonic texture and orchestration, which, although sometimes prefigured in Mahler's earlier works and partly retained in his two later ones, really belongs to this work above all, and is like no other in music.

For the most part, that is. There are, in fact, several layers of feeling in *The Song of the Earth*, which sometimes appear separately and often fuse together inextricably. There is the loneliness mentioned in the letter to Bruno Walter, which dominates the second movement ('The Lonely One in Autumn') and the three 'recitatives' in the finale; also the sensuous hedonistic ecstasy of living, pervasive throughout, and especially prominent in the orchestral central section of the first movement, in the fifth movement ('The Drunkard in Spring'), and in the passage leading up to the funeral march in the finale ('I long, O my friend . . .'). Again, we find a wistful and half amused delight in remembered friendship and beauty, particularly in the third movement ('Youth') and the fourth ('Beauty'); then a sense of the infinite sadness of mortality, again pervasive throughout, notably in the quieter parts of the first movement and finale; and at one point – the hysterical passage about the ape in the first movement – there is the sheer horror that was to break out with full violence in the Ninth Symphony. Finally, at the very end, there is the naked fusion of sadness and ecstasy which is fundamental to the whole work: despite the almost unbearable poignancy of the coda ('The dear earth'), it is at the same time a passionate praise of earthly life in all its overpowering beauty. Music is unique amongst the arts in being able to express several conflicting emotions at the same time, and of no work is this more true than of *The Song of the Earth*.

✳

The first A minor movement, 'The Drinking Song of Earth's Sorrow', voices a furious defiance of grief, which keeps falling into a shadowy subsidiary theme. There is an exquisite central section for orchestra, a shimmering vision of earth's beauty ('The firmament is blue eternally, and the earth will long stand fast and blossom in spring . . .'); and an inconsolable refrain – 'Dark is life, is death'. The ending is uncompromisingly black.

The slow movement, 'The Lonely One in Autumn', evokes a scene of mist and hoar-frost; the poet's weary resignation rises to a great passionate cry 'Sun of love, will you never shine again and dry up, tenderly, my bitter tears?'

The three following movements are contrasted scherzos, in lighter vein, presenting memories of lost joys. 'Youth', a tinkling Allegretto, depicts a little summer-house on an island, with young people chatting and drinking tea, the whole reflected upside-down in the water. 'Beauty', a delicate Andante, portrays young girls gathering flowers; a noisy middle section pictures young horsemen riding by. 'The Drunkard in Spring' is a more robust movement, switching swiftly from key to key, and from a reeling Allegro (the happy drunkard staggering to bed) to a deeply-longing 'nature music' Lento with dreamy bird-calls (the chirruping that tells him of the arrival of spring).

The Adagio finale, 'The Farewell', is by far the longest movement, and the crown of the whole work. The atmosphere is sombre and tragic: a deep booming tam-tam, a stab of pain on the oboe, a melancholy 'marching away' rhythm on horns and clarinets. A 'lonely' narrative passage, with only a flute obbligato over a held double bass note, tells of sunset in the mountains, twilight, and the coolness of night. Later a winding oboe melody evokes murmuring streams; the words speak of night bringing sleep to weary men and beasts. The narrative returns: a solitary figure is waiting for a friend to come and take a last farewell. More murmuring music speaks of separation and passionate longing. Then the sounds of nature fade into silence and darkness, and the opening returns like a stroke of doom, continuing with bursts of dissonant counterpoint which strain the tonality to breaking point. Out of the 'marching away' figure grows a flowing, elegiac funeral march which culminates in a tragic climax. The narrative returns in utter darkness, without the flute obbligato: the friend has arrived and takes his farewell, saying 'I wander in the mountains, I seek rest for my lonely heart! I journey to the homeland, to my resting-place; I shall never again go seeking the far distance. My heart is still and awaits its hour!' Then, in a hushed, broad C major coda, Mahler looks back lovingly at life, to words added to the text by himself: 'The dear earth everywhere blossoms in spring and grows green again. Everywhere and eternally the distance shines bright and blue. Eternally . . . eternally. . . .' The work fades out in unsatisfied longing, the soloist's last 'eternally' floating suspended on the air.

DAS TRINKLIED VOM JAMMER DER ERDE	THE DRINKING SONG OF EARTH'S SORROW
Schon winkt der Wein im gold'nen Pokale,	*Now beckons the wine in the golden goblet,*
Doch trinkt noch nicht, erst sing' ich euch ein Lied!	*But drink not yet, first I'll sing you a song!*
Das Lied vom Kummer	*The song of sorrow*
Soll auflachend in die Seele euch klingen.	*Shall resound in gusts of laughter through your soul.*
Wenn der Kummer naht,	*When sorrow draws near,*
Liegen wüst die Gärten der Seele,	*The gardens of the soul lie wasted,*
Welkt hin und stirbt die Freude, der Gesang.	*Joy and song wither and die.*
Dunkel ist das Leben, ist der Tod.	*Dark is life, and so is death.*

Herr dieses Hauses!
Dein Keller birgt die Fülle des goldenen
  Weins!
Hier, diese Laute nenn' ich mein!
Die Laute schlagen und die Gläser leeren,
Das sind die Dinge, die zusammen passen.
Ein voller Becher Weins zur rechten Zeit
Ist mehr wert, als alle Reiche dieser Erde!
Dunkel ist das Leben, ist der Tod!

Das Firmament blaut ewig, und die Erde
Wird lange fest steh'n und aufblüh'n im
  Lenz.
Du aber, Mensch, wie lang lebst denn du?
Nicht hundert Jahre darfst du dich ergötzen
An all dem morschen Tande dieser Erde!

Seht dort hinab! Im Mondschein auf den
  Gräbern
Hockt eine wild-gespenstische Gestalt.
Ein Aff'ist's! Hört ihr, wie sein Heulen
Hinausgellt in den süssen Duft des Lebens!

Jetzt nehmt den Wein! Jetzt ist es Zeit,
  Genossen!
Leert eure gold'nen Becher zu Grund!
Dunkel ist das Leben, ist der Tod!

(*after Li-Tai-Po*)

Master of this house!
Your cellar holds its fill of golden wine!
Here, this lute I name my own!
To strike the lute and to drain the glasses,
These are the things that go well together.
A full goblet of wine at the right time
Is worth more than all the kingdoms of this
  earth!
Dark is life, and so is death.

The firmament is blue eternally, and the earth
Will long stand fast and blossom in spring.
But you, O man, for how long do you live?
Not for a hundred years can you delight
In all the rotten trash of this earth!

Look down there! In the moonlight, on
  the graves
Squats a mad spectral figure.
It is an ape! Hear how his howling
Screams its way through the sweet fragrance
  of life!

Now take the wine! Now it is time,
  companions!
Drain your golden goblets to the dregs!
Dark is life, and so is death!

DER EINSAME IM HERBST

THE LONELY ONE IN AUTUMN

Herbstnebel wallen bläulich überm See,
Vom Reif bezogen stehen alle Gräser;
Man meint, ein Künstler habe Staub von
  Jade
Über die feinen Blüten ausgestreut.

Der süsse Duft der Blumen ist verflogen;
Ein kalter Wind beugt ihre Stengel nieder.
Bald werden die verwelkten, gold'nen Blätter
Der Lotosblüten auf dem Wasser zieh'n.

Mein Herz ist müde. Meine kleine Lampe
Erlosch mit Knistern, es gemahnt mich an
  den Schlaf.
Ich komm' zu dir, traute Ruhestätte!

Autumn mists drift blue over the lake,
Covered with rime stands every blade of
  grass;
It is as though an artist had strewn dust of
Over the delicate blossoms.   *jade*

The sweet fragrance of the flowers has faded;
A cold wind bows down their stems.
Soon the withered golden petals
Of the lotus-flowers will be floating on the water.

My heart is weary. My little lamp
Has burnt out with a sputter; it puts me in
  mind to sleep.
I come to you, beloved resting-place!

Ja, gib mir Ruh', ich hab' Erquickung not!	*Yes, give me peace, I have need of consolation.*

Ich weine viel in meinen Einsamkeiten.	
Der Herbst in meinem Herzen währt zu lange.	*I weep much in my loneliness.* *The autumn in my heart persists too long.*
Sonne der Liebe, willst du nie mehr scheinen,	*Sun of love, will you never shine again*
Um meine bittern Tränen mild aufzutrocknen?	*And dry up, tenderly, my bitter tears?*

(after Tschang-Tsi)

VON DER JUGEND

YOUTH

Mitten in dem kleinen Teiche	*In the middle of the little pool*
Steht ein Pavillon aus grünem	*Stands a pavilion of green*
Und aus weissem Porzellan.	*And of white porcelain.*

Wie der Rücken eines Tigers	*Like a tiger's back*
Wölbt die Brücke sich aus Jade	*Arches the bridge of jade*
Zu dem Pavillon hinüber.	*Over to the pavilion*

In dem Häuschen sitzen Freunde,	*In the little house friends are sitting,*
Schön gekleidet, trinken, plaudern.	*Beautifully dressed, drinking, chatting;*
Manche schreiben Verse nieder.	*Several are writing verses.*

Ihre seidnen Ärmel gleiten	*Their silken sleeves slip*
Rückwärts, ihre seidnen Mützen	*Backwards, their silken caps*
Hocken lustig tief im Nacken.	*Perch gaily on the back of their necks.*

Auf des kleinen Teiches stiller	*On the little pool's still*
Wasserfläche zeigt sich alles	*Surface everything appears*
Wunderlich im Spiegelbilde.	*Fantastically in a mirror-image.*

Alles auf dem Kopfe stehend	*Everything is standing on its head*
In dem Pavillon aus grünem	*In the pavilion of green*
Und aus weissem Porzellan;	*And white porcelain;*

Wie ein Halbmond steht die Brücke,	*The bridge seems like a half-moon,*
Umgekehrt der Bogen. Freunde,	*Its arch upside-down. Friends,*
Schön gekleidet, trinken, plaudern.	*Beautifully dressed, are drinking, chatting.*

(after Li-Tai-Po)

110

VON DER SCHÖNHEIT

Junge Mädchen pflücken Blumen,
Pflücken Lotosblumen an dem Uferrande.
Zwischen Büschen und Blättern sitzen sie,
Sammeln Blüten in den Schoss und rufen
Sich einander Neckereien zu.

Gold'ne Sonne webt um die Gestalten,
Spiegelt sie im blanken Wasser wider.
Sonne spiegelt ihre schlanken Glieder,
Ihre süssen Augen wider,
Und der Zephir hebt mit Schmeichelkosen
Das Gewebe ihrer Ärmel auf,
Führt den Zauber
Ihrer Wolhgerüche durch die Luft.

O sieh, was tummeln sich für schöne Knaben
Dort an dem Uferrand auf mut'gen Rossen,
Weithin glänzend wie die Sonnenstrahlen;
Schon zwischen dem Geäst der grünen
    Weiden
Trabt das jungfrische Volk einher!

Das Ross des einen wiehert fröhlich auf,
Und scheut, und saust dahin,
Über Blumen, Gräser wanken hin die Hufe,
Sie zerstampfen jäh im Sturm die hinge-
    sunk'nen Blüten.
Hei! Wie flattern im Taumel seine Mähnen,
Dampfen heiss die Nüstern!

Gold'ne Sonne webt um die Gestalten,
Spiegelt sie im blanken Wasser wider.
Und die schönste von den Jungfrau'n sendet
Lange Blicke ihm der Sehnsucht nach.
Ihre stolze Haltung ist nur Verstellung.
In dem Funkeln ihrer grossen Augen,
In dem Dunkel ihres heissen Blicks
Schwingt klagend noch die Erregung ihres
    Herzens nach.

(*after Li-Tai-Po*)

BEAUTY

Young maidens are plucking flowers,
Plucking lotus-flowers by the river's edge.
Amid the bushes and leaves they sit,
Gathering flowers in their laps, and calling
To one another teasingly.

Golden sunlight weaves around their forms,
Mirrors them in the shining water.
Sunlight mirrors their slender limbs
And their sweet eyes,
And the breeze lifts with wheedling caresses
The fabric of their sleeves,
Bears the magic
Of their pleasing fragrance through the air.

O look, racing along, what handsome lads,
There on the river bank, on spirited horses,
Afar-off shining like the sun's rays;
Now between the branches of the green
    willows
They canter along, lads in the flush of
    youth!

The horse of one of them whinnies joyfully,
And shies and tears away,
Over the flowers and the grass his hooves
    are scudding,
Trampling in sudden onslaught the fallen
    flowers.
Hey! Look at its mane flapping frenziedly,
Its nostrils steaming hotly.

Golden sunlight weaves around their forms,
Mirrors them in the shining water.
And the loveliest of the maidens sends
Long glances of yearning after him.
Her proud bearing is only pretence.
In the flashing of her large eyes,
In the darkness of her passionate glance,
The tumult of her heart still surges
    painfully towards him.

DER TRUNKENE IM FRÜHLING

Wenn nur ein Traum das Leben ist,
Warum denn Müh' und Plag'?
Ich trinke, bis ich nicht mehr kann,
Den ganzen lieben Tag!

Und wenn ich nicht mehr trinken kann,
Weil Kehl' und Seele voll,
So tauml' ich bis zu meiner Tür
Und schlafe wundervoll!

Was hör' ich beim Erwachen? Horch!
Ein Vogel singt im Baum.
Ich frag' ihn ob schon Frühling sei,
Mir ist als wie im Traum.

Der Vogel zwitschert: Ja!
Der Lenz ist da, sei kommen über Nacht!
Aus tiefstem Schauen lauscht' ich auf,
Der Vogel singt und lacht!

Ich fülle mir den Becher neu
Und leer' ihn bis zum Grund
Und singe, bis der Mond erglänzt
Am schwarzen Firmament!

Und wenn ich nicht mehr singen kann,
So schlaf' ich wieder ein.
Was geht mich denn der Frühling an?
Lasst mich betrunken sein!

(after Li-Tai-Po)

DRUNKARD IN SPRING

If life is but a dream,
Why then toil and fret?
I drink till I can drink no longer,
The whole livelong day.

And when I can drink no longer,
Since gullet and soul are full,
Then I stagger to my door
And sleep stupendously!

What do I hear when I awake? Listen!
A bird sings in the tree.
I ask him if the spring is here;
I feel as if I were dreaming.

The bird twitters 'Yes!
Spring is here – came overnight!'
In deepest wonder I listen,
The bird sings and laughs!

I fill my glass again,
And drain it to the dregs,
And sing, until the moon shines bright
In the black firmament.

And when I can sing no longer,
Then I go back to sleep;
For what does spring matter to me?
Let me be drunk!

DER ABSCHIED

Die Sonne scheidet hinter dem Gebirge.
In alle Täler steigt der Abend nieder
Mit seinen Schatten, die voll Kühlung sind.
O sieh! Wie eine Silberbarke schwebt
Der Mond am blauen Himmelssee herauf.
Ich spüre eines feinen Windes Weh'n
Hinter den dunklen Fichten!

Der Bach singt voller Wohllaut durch das
    Dunkel.
Die Blumen blassen im Dämmerschein.
Die Erde atmet voll von Ruh' und Schlaf;

THE FAREWELL

The sun is going down behind the mountains.
In every valley evening is descending,
Bringing its shadows, which are full of
    coolness.
O look! like a silver bark
The moon floats up through the blue lake
    of heaven.
I sense a delicate breeze shivering
Behind the dark fir-trees.

The brook sings melodiously through the
    darkness.

Alle Sehnsucht will nun träumen.
Die müden Menschen geh'n heimwärts,
Um im Schlaf vergess'nes Glück
Und Jugend neu zu lernen.
Die Vögel hocken still in ihren Zweigen.
Die Welt schläft ein!

Es wehet kühl im Schatten meiner Fichten.
Ich stehe hier und harre meines Freundes;
Ich harre sein zum Letzten Lebewohl.
Ich sehne mich, O Freund, an deiner Seite
Die Schönheit dieses Abends zu geniessen.
Wo bleibst du! Du lässt mich lang allein!
Ich wandle auf und nieder mit meiner Laute
Auf Wegen, die von weichem Grase
    schwellen.
O Schönheit! O ewigen Liebens-, Lebens-
    trunk'ne Welt!

(*after Mong-Kao-Jen*)

Er stieg vom Pferd und reichte ihm den
    Trunk des Abschieds dar.
Er fragte ihn, wohin er führe
Und auch warum es müsste sein.
Er sprach, seine Stimme war umflort:
Du, mein Freund,
Mir war auf dieser Welt das Glück nicht
    hold!
Wohin ich geh'? Ich geh', ich wand're in die
    Berge.
Ich suche Ruhe für mein einsam Herz!
Ich wandle nach der Heimat, meiner Stätte!
Ich werde niemals in die Ferne schweifen.
Still ist mein Herz und harret seiner Stunde!

Die liebe Erde allüberall
Blüht auf im Lenz und grünt aufs neu!
Allüberall und ewig blauen licht die Fernen!
Ewig ... Ewig ...

(*after Wang-Wei*)

The flowers grow pale in the twilight.
The earth is breathing, full of rest and sleep;
All desire now turns to dreaming.
Weary mortals wend homewards,
So that, in sleep, they may learn anew
Forgotten joy and youth.
The birds huddle silent on their branches.
The world is falling asleep!

A cool breeze blows in the shadow of my
    fir-trees.
I stand here and wait for my friend.
I wait for him to take a last farewell.
I long, O my friend, to be by your side,
To enjoy the beauty of this evening.
Where are you? You leave me long alone!
I wander to and fro with my lute
On pathways which billow with soft grass.
O beauty! O eternal-love-and-life-
    intoxicated world!

He alighted from his horse and handed him
    the drink of farewell.
He asked him where he was going,
And also why it had to be.
He spoke, his voice was veiled:
'Ah! my friend –
Fortune was not kind to me in this world!
Where am I going? I am going to wander
    in the mountains,
I seek rest for my lonely heart!
I journey to the homeland, to my resting-
    place;
I shall never again go seeking the far
    distance.
My heart is still and awaits its hour!'

The dear earth everywhere
Blossoms in spring and grows green again!
Everywhere and forever the distance shines
    bright and blue!
Forever ... forever ...

SYMPHONY No. 9, *composed 1908–11 (mostly 1909); first performed in Vienna, 1912, under Bruno Walter.*
When Mahler completed this symphony, he had to call it No. 9; but he fortified himself with the thought that it was 'really' No. 10 – 'the danger was over'. It is another farewell, but of a more desperate kind: if *The Song of the Earth* implied the idea of death in poetic terms, the Ninth Symphony was a naked encounter with the arch-enemy himself, who invaded the music, turning everything to dust and ashes.

Mahler returned to the purely orchestral symphony in four movements for what was to be his final completed work; but he still used a progressive tonality – the converse of the 'affirmative' one in the Fifth and Seventh Symphonies, moving downwards a semitone. The orchestra is again normal, except for extra wind; the scoring uses both the middle-period hardness and the new rarification of *The Song of the Earth*; the style is a culmination of the tonal disruptions and the 'horror' elements of the Sixth and Seventh Symphonies.

*

The Ninth Symphony is the centrepiece of the last-period trilogy; and like its equivalents in the two earlier ones – the idealistic 'death-and-resurrection' No. 2, and the stoical 'death-without-resurrection' No. 6 – it plunges into a darkness which represents the spiritual nadir of its period. In this last period, however, everything is on a much more extreme plane than before. The Ninth Symphony marks Mahler's furthermost descent into the hell of despair that suddenly confronted him after the mighty spiritual affirmation of No. 8, when he was told by his doctor that he had not long to live, and found his hard-won religious faith too insecure to exorcise the spectre of his swiftly approaching premature extinction. The first symphony of the trilogy, *The Song of the Earth*, is inexpressibly poignant, but it uses purely poetic terms to evoke the shadow of death. And the last symphony, the Tenth, although it too plumbs the depths of despair, rises in the finale above the terror of death and the heart-break of leave-taking, to a calm and transfigured acceptance (this is clear in the final pages of the facsimile of Mahler's manuscript, which is his real 'last musical testament' – not the end of the Ninth, as is so often said.) But in the Ninth, death is confronted on a naked existential plane, and is seen as omnipotent.

As Alban Berg wrote: 'The whole [first] movement is permeated by the premonition of death. Again and again it makes itself felt. All the elements of terrestrial dreaming culminate in it . . . most potently, of course, in the colossal passage where this premonition becomes *certainty* – when in the midst of the deepest and most painful joy in life, death announces itself "with the greatest force".' This phrase, 'with the greatest force', is Mahler's expressive marking over the 'colossal passage' to which Berg refers – the plunge from intense exultation straight into the overwhelming image of death which is the great climax of the movement. The work is, in truth, Mahler's 'dark night of the soul'; and it is all the more moving in that there is no easy yielding to despair. Amid the heartache of the finale, after all the horror and hopelessness of the first three movements, Mahler's unquenched love of life still shines through, thanks to the capacity of great music for expressing contrary feelings simultaneously. The symphony stands as a musical equivalent of the poet Rilke's 'dennoch preisen' – 'praising life in spite of everything'.

But why should we be so specially interested in Mahler's feelings? Certain people are so repelled by what they call the romantic, autobiographical approach to music (even though this was Mahler's own approach), that they have adopted the characteristic present-day attitude of regarding Mahler's Ninth Symphony from a purely aesthetic point of view. A writer recently suggested that the Ninth was not at all Mahler's 'farewell to life' but his 'farewell to the symphony' – which sounds very plausible until we remember that Mahler made it clear that he had *not* taken his farewell of the symphony, by going on to make a comprehensive draft of a five-movement Tenth. Another suggestion is that the Ninth was Mahler's 'farewell to tonality', which again only sounds persuasive until we remember the large areas of music in the work that are absolutely tonal, diatonic and triadic, and the equally large areas of this kind of music in the sketch of the Tenth.

A more intelligent aesthetic approach to the Ninth, which is very widespread, concentrates on the purely 'prophetic' character of its style: its foreshadowing of revolutionary elements in the music of Schoenberg – the occasional breakdown of tonality, and the starkly contrapuntal character of much of the orchestral texture. But the danger here is that we may be led to reduce Mahler to the position of a mere 'forerunner' – just as Mozart was reduced to the position of a mere forerunner of Beethoven during the nineteenth century. And in any case, the historical perspective of such a view is quite wrong: by 1909, the year in which Mahler composed the bulk of the symphony, Schoenberg (no doubt partly influenced by the new elements in Mahler's earlier symphonies) had already, in his *Five Orchestral Pieces* and *Erwartung*, reached a far more advanced position. It should now be possible, nearly three-quarters of a century later, to see Mahler as a great composer in his own right – moving towards his younger contemporary Schoenberg, no doubt, but no more than Mozart was moving towards *his* younger contemporary, Beethoven.

The most valid aesthetic approach to the Ninth, undoubtedly, is that which stresses the work's remarkable originality in relation to the symphonic tradition. There is the constant variation of themes, the continual interpenetration of one theme by another, and the uniquely subtle and far-reaching treatment of 'cyclic' form: the latter not only in the reworking in the finale of material from the second movement and Rondo-Burleske, but also in the use of a disruptive modulatory sequence, initiated in the second movement, to permeate the rest of the symphony. Indeed, the strange modulation itself is already introduced in a simple form in the first movement: here, Mahler manifestly refers to the opening theme of Beethoven's 'Les Adieux' Piano Sonata (Beethoven's second statement of the theme, where he himself gives it a flat-submediant modulation).

Again, there is the unorthodox disposition of the four traditional types of movement. The first is not the customary Allegro, but an Andante containing Allegro elements; and after the second movement has followed one tradition by being a scherzo in dance-rhythm, the third movement again flouts tradition by being another scherzo, in rapid march-rhythm, which moreover has the size and brilliance of the customary finale. But the finale itself is an Adagio – a procedure no doubt derived from Haydn's Forty-fifth and Tchaikovsky's Sixth (both 'farewell' symphonies, we may remember) – but *this* 'farewell' finale sums up the whole symphony in a quite unprecedented way. Apart from anything else – its 'cyclic' character, for instance – it gives the symphony its 'progressive tonality'; after the keys of the first three movements – D major, C major and A minor – it turns, not to the D major demanded by tradition, but to D *flat* major.

Yet such technical, aesthetic exegesis tells us nothing about the work's actual nature. A symphony could be composed, fitting all the above descriptions, which would be completely different from Mahler's Ninth. What is the point, for example, of the finale being an Adagio, in a key a semitone lower than that of the first movement? The point, surely, is the extraordinary emotional character of the music itself – a three-sided conflict between agonized despair, a deep love of life, and a resigned sense of valediction – a character confirmed by its hushed, long-drawn quotation, just before the end, of the final vocal phrase of one of Mahler's own *Kindertotenlieder*, a phrase which pictures the dead children transfigured 'upon the heights'.

Are we then thrown back on to the autobiographical approach after all? Not in the least, since the 'subjective' feelings a great composer expresses, it goes without saying, are conceived by him as being those of Everyman. If, as we are often told, Mahler is too much concerned with himself in his music, why does it strike so many sympathetic chords in so many other people's hearts?

*

The opening Andante, in D, has a few preludial bars stating some main ideas in ghostly orchestral colours: a halting rhythm in the bass (like a faltering heart-beat); a tolling bell-figure on harp; a sad phrase on muted horn; a rustling, or palpitation, on violas. Against this background the violins introduce the main theme, a warm singing melody redolent of summer, full of tender longing: but a dark shadow has fallen across the Austrian summer which has been the permanent setting of Mahler's hours of fulfilment. The movement is a conflict between this main theme and a tormented, chromatic idea in D minor, which breaks in with bitter protest. The main theme, returning, rises to a painfully aspiring climax, crowned with a tragic fanfare for trumpets, to burst out in great downward-swooping intervals of defiant joy. The two ideas now alternate three times; each time, before the main theme returns, a mighty climax wrings jubilation from despair by introducing a new theme, full of 'all-or-nothing' exultation. The first climax is followed by menacing, grotesque, dissonant references to the introductory bars. The second and third climaxes result in catastrophic collapses; the third reaches breaking point, the halting rhythm and the bell-figure thundering out on trombones and timpani like a dreadful summons. The outcome is a funeral march rhythm, out of which the main theme struggles back, shockingly disfigured and distorted. Finally a wandering cadenza for solo instruments, like a maze of shadows, leads to a quiet coda, in which the 'exultant' theme is played sadly by solo horn – an echo of what might have been; the movement disintegrates into thin air.

In the two central movements, bitterness and horror run riot. The scherzo, in C, is a Ländler – a Ländler divested of all charm, life and significance, presenting the 'dance of life' as something utterly tawdry, stupid and empty. The main material comprises simple dance elements scored with ghastly dryness, phrased leeringly, and made to trip awkwardly over one another. The first trio is a distorted waltz, with brutally vulgar trombone deliveries of cheap, popular-style melodies. These two ideas alternate and intermingle, eventually disrupting the tonality with swift chains of flat-submediant key-switches, which will permeate the rest of the symphony. Only in the second trio, a gently nostalgic type of Ländler, does peace return for a moment or two, but this is submerged by the 'tawdry' music, which fades away at the end like a phantom.

The Rondo-Burleske, in A minor, is Mahler's most modern movement: a masterly structure of dissonant linear counterpoint, a contrived chaos built from a myriad of fragments of theme, a ferocious outburst of fiendish laughter at the futility of everything. Out of the vicious introductory fragments a first group emerges, 'crazy' music made up of rapid vehement motives combined in rhythmically disjointed counterpoints. A wild, wryly modulating march offers a chance of comparative stability, but is swept away in the general uproar. The second group is a sort of demented band music, using the disruptive modulatory sequence of the scherzo. The two sections alternate; the first group, on later appearances, adds a shrill atonal figure on woodwind like a lewd grimace. Suddenly the pandemonium is stilled by a visionary episode in D, which looks back to the key and near serenity of the first movement's main theme. The material of this episode is the 'lewd grimace', given a calm diatonic dignity by the trumpet, and later transformed by the violins into a passionate theme of supreme beauty. But the main material, after several unavailing attempts, breaks in again, and ends the movement in the devilish mood in which it began.

The Adagio finale, in D flat, transmutes horror and bitterness into courage-ous acceptance and unquenched belief in life, musically as well as emotionally. The noble, hymn-like main theme, built out of transfigured versions of the distorted material of the Burleske, pours out passionately Mahler's intense love of life; riddled through with the disruptive modulatory sequence, it sweeps forward unflinchingly, its tonality unscathed. For its middle strain, it refashions the tragic fanfare from the first movement, as a kind of brave insistence on joy from out of the midst of suffering. The second group, in the minor, spanning the heights and depths of pitch with a sparse two- and three-part texture, combines contrapuntally a few wisps of disembodied theme, utterly empty of feeling – 'all passion spent'. Passion (the first group) breaks in again, however, and alternates several times with this resigned music, each time growing in intensity. After a heartbreaking climax on the brass (the tragic fanfare), it makes one final *fortissimo* affirmation, before beginning a slow, lingering fade-out. Casting a long, steadfast look back at life, it fades into the distance, full of a profound peace.

SYMPHONY NO. 10 IN F SHARP, *sketched 1910; first and third move-ments edited by Křenek, with additions by Franz Schalk and/or Alexander von Zemlinsky, first performed in Vienna, 1924, under Schalk; performing version by Deryck Cooke first broadcast (incomplete) 1960, conducted by Berthold Goldschmidt; first complete performance London, 1964, under Goldschmidt; full score (incorporating a complete transcription of the sketch) published 1976.*

Death accepted Mahler's numbering, cutting him off, like Beethoven, with his Tenth Symphony unfinished. But Mahler got further than Beethoven. As it stands, the work is a five-movement symphony, a practically unbroken flow of music from beginning to end; unfortunately, for long periods the texture is extremely sketchy, in places almost non-existent. It is obvious that the score, and probably the whole conception, was due for a good deal of revision. Nevertheless, it shows clearly that Mahler, far from plunging further into preoccupation with death, was moving towards a more vitally creative attitude.

✳

When Mahler began his Tenth Symphony, in 1910, he followed his habitual procedure. He first built up a full-length sketch of the whole work in four-stave score (looking rather like a piano-duet layout), with indications as to certain important features of the intended orchestration. The result was five folders, each containing a movement continuous from beginning to end –

118

though due to haste, continuity was preserved in places by a single thematic line only, and in one movement by a 'da capo' indication.

Then followed the second stage – the elaboration of this four-stave sketch into a full-score draft. But about halfway through this process Mahler died, leaving only three folders to represent this stage – drafts of two full-length movements, and of the first thirty bars of another. And so he did not even begin the third stage – the elaboration of the full-score draft into the final definitive full score of the completed work. He had, however, decided on the order of the movements, having written blue-pencil roman numerals on the covers of five of the folders. They are as follows:

I. A folder entitled 'Adagio', containing a full-score draft of a movement in F sharp major. This had advanced so far towards its final state that it can be played practically as it stands. However, from about halfway through there are manifest deficiencies: tempo indications, expressive markings, dynamics and phrasing are lacking, and the woodwind staves are suspiciously empty for long periods.

II. A folder entitled '2. Scherzo – Finale', containing a full-score draft of a movement in F sharp minor moving to major. The movement does have something of the character of a finale; and indeed it would seem that at one stage Mahler had thought of placing the fourth movement – the cover of which bears the crossed-out title '1. Scherzo (I. Satz)' [1st scherzo (1st movement)] – first, and this movement last. The state of this full-score sketch is not nearly as advanced as that of the Adagio: the main thematic sections – the opening main scherzo material, the pastoral first trio, and the waltz-like second trio – can be played practically as they stand, but elsewhere the scoring is sketched in for strings and brass only, even for first violins and brass, and sometimes there is a thematic line on one stave only. There are no tempo indications after the initial one, no expressive markings, and hardly any dynamics or phrasing. However, some of these things can be supplied from the four-stave sketch of the movement, including harmonic textures which Mahler had not carried over.

III. A folder entitled 'No. 3. Purgatorio', containing a four-stave sketch of a movement in B flat minor and a full-score draft of the first thirty bars of the same movement. In the four-stave sketch, after the central section, a return to the opening is begun, followed by the words 'da capo' and a coda. The fragment of full-score sketch can be played as it stands; and the four-stave sketch, which has scarcely any textural deficiencies, is littered with indications of the intended orchestration.

IV. A folder without title, containing a four-stave sketch of a movement progressing from E minor to D minor, with no tempo indications at all, but with the manifest character of a scherzo. The texture is fairly full throughout, but it becomes deficient at times in the central section; and later on, recapitulations of earlier passages are indicated by the thematic line only.

Dynamic markings are often lacking, and there are very few indications of the intended orchestration: this and the following movement were obviously written down in great haste.

v. A folder marked 'Finale', containing a four-stave sketch of a movement with an Introduction in D minor (without tempo indication), a D minor Allegro moderato, and a long coda (again without tempo indication) which leads the symphony back to its original key of F sharp major. The textural state of the movement is more complete than that of the preceding one, but again there are few indications of the intended orchestration.

These five folders, the first two collated with the equivalent four-stave sketches, are the basis of my performing version. The above description of the manuscript shows clearly that this performing version cannot in any way be thought of as an intended completion of the symphony, as some people have suggested. If Mahler had lived to complete the work, he would have elaborated the music considerably, refined and perfected it in a thousand details, possibly expanded or contracted or switched around a passage here or there, and of course clothed it in orchestral sound of a subtlety and vividness beyond all our conjectures.

On the other hand, there is no need to maintain, as certain distinguished Mahlerians do, that my score cannot claim to represent the Tenth Symphony in any sense whatever. It does represent, in simple fact, the stage that the Tenth Symphony had reached when Mahler died. Admittedly, one or two notes are conjectural; and for practical performing reasons certain details have been added – an occasional chord, harmonic progression, bass line, or counter-theme (based on Mahler's own motives). And again, Mahler's own harmonies have been brought back and adapted in those few places where he indicated recapitulation by a single thematic line only; while in the last three movements, the whole orchestration has had to be supplied by trying to divine Mahler's implicit general intentions. Yet the only valid question is this: given that there can never be any such thing as Mahler's own final, definitive score of his Tenth Symphony, does his fairly comprehensive sketch of it, put into score by other hands, provide a Mahlerian experience of any real value? My own belief is that it does, simply because Mahler's actual *music*, even in its unrevised and unelaborated state, has such strength and beauty that it dwarfs into insignificance the few momentary uncertainties about notes and the subsidiary additions, and even survives being presented in conjectural orchestration. After all, the leading thematic line throughout, and something like ninety per cent of the counterpoint and harmony, are pure Mahler, and vintage Mahler at that.

*

The opening Adagio in F sharp, which is complete, follows the pattern of the finale of the Ninth, but in a more positive way: the main theme is again passionate and riddled with dissonance, but it rises assertively in big leaping intervals; the second group is again resigned, but keeps breaking into protest; the climax is not heartbreak, but a massive organ-like chant culminating in a terrifying dissonance (a nine-note chord), like some awe-inspiring cosmic revelation. After this, a feeling of valediction does enter the music, but of a more serene kind.

The scherzo, in F sharp minor, sketched in full score, shows Mahler looking not back but forward. There is a new taut power in the first group; the mood is fierce but sane, without a trace of the madness of the Burleske in the Ninth. The second group consists of lively, genial, pastoral music in F; the trio is a joyful E flat Ländler, a radiant reincarnation of Mahler's favourite dance form, after its dessication in the Ninth; the conclusion is a powerful combination of the pastoral and Ländler themes in F sharp major, with a final 'shout for joy'. This music speaks of life, not of death.

The brief B flat minor movement entitled 'Purgatorio' is a pathetic little piece, using the 'treadmill' ostinato from the song 'Das irdische Leben', with sunny interludes and a sudden passionate outburst of supplication.

The rest is roughed out in short score. The fourth movement (E minor to D minor) alternates passionate lament with limping waltz music, which eventually dies away in the 'horror' vein, with a final loud stroke on muffled bass drum; the 'death' mood is back, and continues in the opening of the finale.

The finale's form is Adagio–Allegro–Adagio. The Adagio, opening in D minor, picks up the muffled drum-stroke, repeating it like a 'blow of fate' amidst sombre music in the bass register; but out of this rises a long-drawn lyrical melody of strange, unearthly beauty, which progresses tonally through D major to B major. Soaring to an impassioned climax, it is cut off in midstream by the drum-stroke, and the sombre music returns to D minor. This key is continued by the Allegro, a savage, 'crazy' affair recalling to some extent the Burleske of the Ninth; the music rises to a shattering climax – the dissonant chord from the first movement. But the soaring lyrical melody returns, continuing its way as if never interrupted, to end the symphony in its true key of F sharp, with a sigh of great tenderness. This is not the music of death, but – as is confirmed by Mahler's avowal of devotion to his wife written over the last bars – of love. There was still plenty of life left in Mahler when death claimed him: the Tenth Symphony reveals that the Ninth had been a phase, like the Sixth, which he had faced and overcome.

WHAT Mahler had to say is of particular importance, because of what he said it in the teeth of. We might compare his report on experience with Edmund Blunden's, set down in his poem of that name:

> I have been young, and now am not too old;
> And I have seen the righteous forsaken,
> His health, his honour and his quality taken.
>> This is not what we were formerly told.
>
> I have seen a green country, useful to the race,
> Knocked silly with guns and mines, its villages vanished,
> Even the last rat and last kestrel banished –
>> God bless us all, this was peculiar grace.
>
> I knew Seraphina; Nature gave her hue,
> Glance, sympathy, note, like one from Eden.
> I saw her smile warp, heard her lyric deaden;
>> She turned to harlotry; – this I took to be new.
>
> Say what you will, our God sees how they run.
> These disillusions are His curious proving
> That He loves humanity and will go on loving;
>> Over there are faith, life, virtue in the sun.

The report of a puzzled Englishman, reasserting against the grim realities of life the faith of his fathers. Mahler was just as puzzled: he had not seen war, but he had only too realistically imagined it; and he had seen too much madness, suicide and early death. What is worse, he had a destructive inner stress, which he could not resolve by asserting an inherited faith. He delved deep into the horror of life; he was forced to confront, with a divided and tormented mind, a possible ultimate nihilism. Yet through all his gruesome revelations of the abyss shine his love and praise of life, his noble and unquenched courage, and above all his utter integrity and fidelity to the truth

123

– as he saw it. His report on experience, taken as a whole, may seem a disquieting one, but it was a true one, his own – could it have been anyone else's? And in the end he too could say with Blunden: 'Over there are faith, life, virtue in the sun'.

INDEX